The
TOUCH
of the
MASTER

Extraordinary stories
of how God is using
ordinary men and women
and an international mission
called
Operation Mobilization

By Deborah Meroff

**OM Literature
P.O. Box 1047
129 Mobilization Drive
Waynesboro, GA 30830-2047, U.S.A.**

Title: **The Touch of the Master**
Extraordinary stories of how God is using ordinary men and
women and an international mission called Operation Mobilization

Published by OM Literature
P.O. Box 1047, Waynesboro, GA 30830-2047 USA

**All royalties and profits from the sale of this book will go back
into missions.**

OM FIELD ADDRESSES:

OM AUSTRALIA
P.O. Box 32,
Box Hill, VIC 3128

OM CANADA
212 West Street,
Port Colborne, Ontario L3K 4E3

OM INDIA
P.O. Box No. 2014,
Secunderabad 500 003

OM NETHERLANDS
Postbus 390
(Lange Nering 13)
NL-8300 AJ Emmeloord

OM NEW ZEALAND
P.O. Box 914
Papakura 1730

OM SHIPS
Postfach 1565
D-74819 Mosbach

OM UNITED KINGDOM
The Quinta
Weston Rhyn
OSWESTRY
Shropshire SY10 7LT

OM USA
P.O. Box 444
Tyrone, GA 30290

ISBN 18845-4310-3

Printed in Colombia
Impreso en Colombia

Foreword

It is hard to believe that 40 years have passed since Operation Mobilization began with three of us college students traveling to Mexico. Since then approximately 100,000 people have served and trained with OM in more than 80 nations around the world. We have seen amazing answers to prayer along the way. Of course, there also have been heartbreaks and disappointments. For decades people have been asking us for a book about OM. Praise God, thanks to Debbie Meroff, we now have one. I hope these true stories of real events in Operation Mobilization around the globe will bless you and help you to be a better intercessor for God's work. The chapters of our Master's amazing grace and provision to OM continue to be written. He reaches out to men and women everywhere, seeking to heal and transform lives. His touch is for us all. And He delights in employing everyone who is willing to build His Kingdom.

To God be the glory!

George Verwer
Founder and International Coordinator
Operation Mobilization

Table of Contents

HIS
COMFORTING
TOUCH

1

The Parable of the Old Man Who Wanted to Get to the Bathroom

by Doug Nichols

While serving with Operation Mobilization in India in 1967, I spent several months in a TB sanatorium with tuberculosis. After finally being admitted into the sanatorium, I tried to give tracts to the patients, doctors and nurses, but no one would take them. You could tell that they weren't really happy with me, a rich American (to them all Americans were rich), being in a government-free sanatorium. They didn't know that serving with OM, I was just as broke as they were!

I was quite discouraged with being sick, everyone angry with me, not being able to witness because of the language barrier, and no one even bothering to take a tract or Gospel of John. The first few nights, I would wake around 2:00 a.m. coughing. One morning as I was going through my coughing spell, I noticed one of the older (and certainly sicker) patients across the aisle trying to get out of bed. He would sit up on the edge of the bed and try to stand, but because of weakness would fall back into bed. I really didn't understand what was happening or what he was trying to do. He finally fell back into bed exhausted. I then heard him begin to cry softly.

9

The next morning I realized what the man was trying to do. He was simply trying to get up and walk to the bathroom! Because of his sickness and extreme weakness he was not able to do this, and being so ill he simply went to the toilet in the bed.

The next morning the stench in our ward was awful. Most of the other patients yelled insults at the man because of the bad smell. The nurses were extremely agitated and angry because they had to clean up the mess, and moved him roughly from side to side to take care of the problem. One of the nurses, in her anger, even slapped him. The man, terribly embarrassed, just curled up into a ball and wept.

The next night, also around 2:00 o'clock, I again woke up coughing. I noticed the man across the aisle sit up again, trying to make his way to the washroom. However, still being so weak he fell back whimpering just as the night before. I'm just like most of you; I don't like bad smells. I didn't want to become involved. I was sick myself. But before I realized what had happened, not knowing why I did it, I got out of my bed and went over to the old man. He was still crying and did not hear me approach. As I reached down and touched his shoulder, his eyes opened with a fearful questioning look. I simply smiled, put my arm under his head and neck, and my other arm under his legs, and picked him up.

Even though I was sick and weak, I was certainly stronger than him. He was extremely light because of his old age and advanced TB. I walked down the hall to the washroom, which was really just a smelly, filthy small room with a hole in the floor. I stood behind him with my arms under his arms, holding him so he could take care of himself. Afterwards I picked him up and carried him back to his bed. As I began to lay him down, with my head next to his, he kissed me on the cheek, smiled, and said something which I supposed was a thank you.

It was amazing what happened the next morning. One of the other patients who I didn't know woke me around 4:00 o'clock with a steaming cup of delicious Indian tea. He then made motions with his hands (he knew no English), indicating he wanted a tract. As the sun came up, some of the other patients began to approach, motioning that they would also like one of the booklets I had tried to distribute before. Throughout the day people came to me, asking for the Gospel booklets. This included the nurses, the hospital interns, the doctors, until everybody in the hospital had a tract, booklet or Gospel of John. Over the next days, several indicated they had trusted Christ as Savior as a result of reading the Good News!

What did it take to reach these people with the Good News of salvation in Christ? It certainly wasn't health. It definitely wasn't the ability to speak or to give an intellectually moving discourse. Health, ability to communicate cross-culturally and sensitiveness to other cultures and peoples are all very important. But what did God use to open their hearts to the Gospel? I simply took an old man to the bathroom. Anyone could have done that!

2

Prison Presence

by Julyan Lidstone

*L*ate September is a great time of year in Ankara, Turkey. Sunshine warms the days but it isn't uncomfortably hot. People relax as they recover from the torrid summer and prepare for the freezing winter.

Late one Saturday afternoon I squeezed off the crowded minibus, crossed over the dusty street to our building and wearily climbed the stairs to the door of our apartment. As I opened the door, an American family visiting us met me. *"They're here!"* they said nervously, and my heart skipped a beat. In the living room were two policemen waiting to arrest me.

"Come down to the police headquarters," was all they said. "We want to ask you some questions."

1988 had been a tough year for all evangelical Christians in Turkey. Back in January and February the tabloid press had run a lurid campaign against us. We read headlines like *'Missionaries Poison our Youth'*. I had personally been accused of luring susceptible young men to our annual Bible camp with promises of English lessons, visas to travel abroad and even foreign wives. When I read that article my stomach tied itself in knots. I knew it was just a matter of time before the police launched an investigation.

Eventually they arrested some believers who were printing evangelistic literature in a Black Sea town. One of them had an address book with the names and addresses of around fifty missionaries and national believers.

Those fifty names represented just about all the evangelicals living outside Istanbul. With a population of around 60 million, Turkey has been aptly described as the 'largest unevangelized nation', and our tiny fellowships were minute drops in a sea of Islam. Missionaries were often deported when caught sharing their faith, and the tragically few national believers lived in constant fear of what might happen if they were arrested. Although the secular constitution guaranteed freedom of religion, fierce social pressures meant a convert from Islam to Christianity could lose his job, be thrown out of his family, or face mocking and ridicule by friends. It is no wonder many that came to faith found they could not stand the pressures, and fell away. Our fragile group of fifteen or so believers were often disillusioned when another eager newcomer suddenly turned against us and stopped attending meetings.

Around the country, the police started a systematic round up and interrogation of the fifty people listed in the address book. Waiting for our turn in Ankara was a time of tension; every Sunday we sang our favorite song, *'Don't Be Afraid'*, over and over again. Towards the end of March there was a knock at our door and a plain-clothes detective asked me to come outside for a few minutes. He then bundled me into a taxi and took me off to the city police headquarters. I was locked up by myself in a small cubicle. Soon, however, I realized the other cubicles contained a dozen others from the Ankara fellowship, both Turkish and expatriate.

That night our homes were searched, and we were subjected to hours of interrogation. The police were determined to get to the bottom of this new "cult", to find out where our center was and where our money came from. They were convinced we had massive amounts of foreign currency pouring in from either the CIA or the KGB, who wanted to destabilize Turkey by creating restive minority groups. It made answering their questions rather easy. All we had to do was tell the truth!

The police pounced on a notebook that detailed how we spent the fellowship's meager collections.

"What's this 50 lira (about £2) for?" My interrogator demanded.

"That was to help someone with their bus fare for coming to the meeting."

"No, it wasn't!" he snarled. "It's code for 50 *thousand* lira to make him convert to Christianity!"

"We haven't got money like that. Just look at the simple houses we live in."

"Ha! That's all a front."

After a couple of days we were released pending trial, and we filled our days working on a defense with our young lawyer. We were being accused of making financial and political gain out of our faith, under a law designed to keep Islamic extremists and imposters in check. Again it made our task easier, as clearly the Turkish believers had lost rather than gained career opportunities and profitable jobs because of their faith. There was a wave of worldwide prayer on our behalf, and when we finally got to the court the judge was quite helpful. In just a couple of hearings we were all acquitted, just like our friends facing similar charges in other cities. What a relief! We were so busy congratulating each other, laughing and hugging, that the court attendants had to move us on to make space for the next case.

But our troubles weren't over yet. The Ankara police chief had a grudge against us and was looking for an opportunity to drag us all in again. "I'm going to keep arresting you all till you are dust!" was his threat. A printer's complaint about an unpaid bill provided the pretext, and so, at the end of September, we were arrested again. This time the aim was not to gather information but to harass and intimidate. The Turkish believers were picked up in a raid on a wedding party, so the bride and groom spent their wedding night behind bars.

This time we were all taken to the basement of the police headquarters. Everyone knew the basement was where leftists were tortured — some never came out alive. The Turkish fellows were taken away one by one, blindfolded, then punched and kicked around a room by four or five policemen for half an hour or so. One of the girls was handcuffed and blindfolded, then led around the corridors until she was shoved into a chair. The chair, she was told, stood on the edge of a swimming pool.

"If you do not tell us all the names of your group we'll push you in," they threatened.

We three foreigners, two Brits and an American, were kept in a cell without light. On the cement floor were bits of cardboard to sleep on. Since none of us had toothbrushes or razors we all felt very rough after a couple of days. We debated how long our confinement would last. "Lord," we prayed, "get us out of here!"

After a couple of days a disheveled prisoner was brought to our cell. Haydar was a bulldozer driver. Every night at midnight he was taken away, and a few hours later he would be led back.

"What happened to you?" we asked him anxiously the first night.

"They tied my arms behind my back and then lifted me off the floor by my arms — it was agony!"

"What did they do that for?"

"Some years ago my brother was killed in a shoot-out with the police," he explained. "They want me to confess that I supplied him with the gun he was using."

We felt very sorry for Haydar and prayed with him for justice and an end to the torture. It put our own situation in a different light. Perhaps the Lord wanted us to minister to others where we were.

The next day we foreigners were taken to a cell with a light and joined by our Turkish brothers. Then a group of leftists were also put into our cell. We got on quite well together, as we had a mutual respect and sympathy for others who suffered for their principles. As a result we had many opportunities to explain our faith as we whiled away the hours. Of course, we also had to listen to lectures on Marxist dogma! The little cell was now packed. When we all lay down on the floor to sleep at night we were jammed in so tightly we couldn't even turn over. The other problem was that the leftists were all chain smokers. The cell had no window or ventilation so we had to plead with the guards to open the door for fresh air every now and again. By this time we were fifteen or so unwashed bodies stinking of tobacco smoke.

How long was this going to go on? We talked, prayed and then talked some more, endlessly trying to guess what was going on and when we would get out. The guards enjoyed playing games with us.

"All right everyone, get up, comb your hair. You're on your way out!" a policeman suddenly shouted with a laugh.

We leapt up, grabbed our few possessions and marched out of the cell and up the stairs to the ground floor. Then we saw the press photographers and TV cameras. Our hearts sank as we realized we were going to be paraded like terrorist suspects. Also on display was a pile of books the police had confiscated from us: our perfectly legal Bibles. The aim was to disgrace and shame us, and make sure that all our families, neighbors and employers knew what we were up to. As we stood there we imagined the whole nation watching us on the news that evening. Since by this time we all looked just like a bunch of criminals, we dreaded the abuse and scorn we would attract from unsympathetic friends and relatives.

Our hopes had been lifted only to be shattered. We felt discouraged and forlorn. Then one of the Turkish believers smiled.

"Cheer up! Look what I pinched from the pile of literature!" Triumphantly he pulled a New Testament from under his jacket. We were never so glad to get God's Word, and eagerly took turns reading it to strengthen our faith.

The next day there was a power cut. Down in the basement we were plunged into utter darkness. After trying to keep a perfunctory conversation going for a while most of us dropped off to sleep. I was left alone with the Lord.

"How long will we be here? What will happen to my family?" I pleaded with Him.

And I heard His response very clearly: "Why are you so worried about your family? Am I not able to look after them?"

I felt ashamed. As I sat in the darkness I surrendered myself and my family to God's will, feeling a strange peace fill me. The confidence came assuring me that whatever happened to us, the Lord was still in control.

At midnight Haydar was taken away as usual. He came back just ten minutes later.

"What happened?" we demanded, concerned. "Why are you back so quickly?"

He beamed. "Oh, they just offered me a cigarette and told me my interrogation is over!"

Together we gave thanks to the Lord for having looked after Haydar and protecting him from signing a forced confession. If Haydar was now in the clear, did that mean our reason for being here had also come to an end?

The next morning the guards were noisily trying to open our cell door. They had received orders to present us to the Public Prosecutor, but they couldn't unlock our door — the officer on the night shift had put our cell keys in his pocket and gone home with them! We listened with amusement as they tried one key and then another with no success. A police headquarters has a lot of keys! In the end they had to give up and unceremoniously smash the lock with an iron bar. When God says it's time to go, no one keeps you in! The crowning touch of that morning came when Haydar asked if he could pray with us. Our hearts overflowed as we listened to him ask the Lord for salvation.

The Public Prosecutor politely asked us a few questions. He then announced he saw no reason to keep us in custody and would release us until he decided whether to bring charges or not. Another anxious wait! Would we have to face another trial?

Just a week later I was amazed to meet the same Public Prosecutor at the door of our flat.

"What are you doing here, sir?" I asked politely.

He replied that he was looking for the caretaker. That made me even more curious.

"And why do you want to see the caretaker!"

"My central heating is leaking!"

It appeared that the same Public Prosecutor who was dealing with our case had just moved into our block of apartments, of all the blocks in that city of several million! Encouraged by this obvious piece of divine intervention, I asked the man the status of our case.

"Don't worry," he responded reassuringly. "You'll be all right."

We were free! Our case had been dropped, and the church in Ankara had come through another trial.

It was only later that we learnt another side to the story. The Ankara correspondent of the British broadsheet newspaper *The Independent* told us how we had become the subjects of international diplomacy. According to international law, a consul always has the right to meet with citizens of his country who have been detained by the police. The woman working at the British Consulate in Ankara at that time had come down to the police headquarters to see us. The police denied we were there, or that they had any knowledge of us. The consul sent a telex about the situation to the Foreign Office in London, who responded with a protest to the Turkish government. The case was discussed at Turkish cabinet level and the Ministry of Foreign Affairs stated that he deplored the harassment of Christians — just the sort of thing guaranteed to make very poor publicity in Europe, at a time when Turkey was hoping to join the European Community. The Ankara police were ordered to stop mistreating Christians. And since then, the Ankara fellowship has indeed enjoyed peace and growth.

The prison incident was the beginning of a new freedom and boldness in the Turkish church. Today there are fellowships of Muslim-background believers worshipping openly in public in four or the main cities of Turkey. Typically they rent an office or shop, inform the local government and explain what is going on to the neighbors. Another breakthrough has been the number of believers who state their faith on their identity cards. Whereas changing from "Muslim" to "Christian" used to be considered too dangerous a move; it is now quite common.

The Turkish church is still very small, but it is growing. The city of Ankara now has around a hundred followers of Christ. Many others in the country have also fought and suffered their battles of faith. But we believe those dark days in the police headquarters in 1988 were part of the story of how God is drawing Turkey to Himself.

3

A Song in the Slums

by James Heard

"Yes, Jesus loves me! Yes, Jesus loves me...."

The song echoed through the squalid slum, reaching the ears of a curious eight-year-old. Ramu tracked down the music's source and soon he was singing along with the other children at a Sunday school run by the OM India team.

After a few weeks, however, the boy began to question the meaning of the words. *"If Jesus really loves me, why doesn't he help me with my problem?"* he wondered.

Ramu was born with a harelip, a malformation of the upper lip. If the condition goes untreated, the nose and mouth become progressively distorted. By the time a child reaches maturity, the lip and nostril widen into a fixed and repulsive deformity. Other children laughed at Ramu and made his life miserable. He approached the OM team with his question.

The workers responded with compassion and took him to see a doctor. After examining the boy the doctor said that a simple operation could rectify the harelip. The problem was money. An operation would cost $40 — an impossible amount for Ramu's parents. As rag pickers they spent twelve to fifteen

21

hours a day sifting through the dumps and scrap heaps of the city, searching for rags they might sell for $2 or $3. This was barely enough to feed the family.

The OM-ers decided to present the need to their churches. An offering was taken for Ramu, and enough was raised for the operation. The boy was thrilled. At long last the eagerly anticipated day arrived, and the surgery was performed without complications.

After a few days Ramu had his first photograph taken — with the biggest smile in the world. In the weeks that followed, the boy and his family all asked Jesus Christ into their lives and became regular attendees of the church in the slums. Now, whenever Ramu sings "Yes, Jesus loves me," he has no doubts whatsoever. Jesus had proved how much He cares. He had heard a boy's cry and healed him, body and soul.

4

Father Heart

by Alfy Franks

*I*n the city of Bombay there are over 300,000 prostitutes. About 60% of them have been kidnapped from other places in India or Nepal and literally sold into the flesh trade. Today, young girls between 11 and 13 fetch around £2,000 in Bombay. Once these children are sold into brothels, they are confined like prisoners, many of them without clothes so they cannot escape. They are forced to satisfy the lust of rich customers who will pay any amount of money for virgins or young girls, in the belief they will renew their youth.

Our teams in Bombay, very much burdened about this situation, asked one of our former OM girls to work with these women. Naomi was very effective and was able to take many girls back to their homes in the south after they were rescued.

There were two rescue homes Naomi visited constantly. After she led these girls to the Lord Jesus Christ she found their parents and their families, and sent them back home. But although some people believed OM had a huge work among Bombay's prostitutes, we were not really even scratching the surface.

One time a father and his younger son came to us from Kathmandu, Nepal. The man told us that his daughter and another girl, both about 14 years old, had been taken by an old man in Kathmandu under the pretext that he was going to find jobs for them in India. Of course, the girls were sold into brothels in Bombay. When the man was finally apprehended by the police, he confessed what he had done.

One of the churches in Kathmandu who knew us wrote to the girl's father and assured him that if he went to see the OM India people, they would find his daughter. So with great hope and expectation this father arrived at our office in Bombay.

I felt like the king to whom Naaman applied for the healing of leprosy. I said in despair, "How in the world can I find your little daughter among 300,000 prostitutes? — and in a place where their keepers have such a terrible power over them that it is impossible even for police to penetrate their strongholds?"

Anyhow, we told the story to Naomi and she went to see another social worker that is a believer. They went about making inquiries to see what they could do. We were discouraged, but we kept on praying that God would have mercy upon this father. As a father myself, I knew the agony that he was going through.

It was during the course of one afternoon, when he and a few others were walking up and down the street in a red light area, praying, that something made him stop and look up. His eyes focused on a window of an upper story building. And there, beyond all hope or reason, he recognized his own daughter looking down at him. The girl immediately signaled him not to make any disturbance, but to go back and inform the police. Her father found Naomi and she and the social worker went to the authorities.

By the time the police got to the house, the girl had been tied up and hidden. Finally, however, by God's grace, she was rescued. She later described how desperate she had become.

That afternoon she was sleeping on her bed when suddenly she heard a voice tell her distinctly to go and look out of the window. She obeyed, and the next moment sighted her father walking down the street. When he stopped and looked up she was almost overcome.

The father very naturally wanted to take his children home at once, but Naomi restrained him. She convinced him that the gang would see that he didn't even reach the railway station alive. Naomi went back to the police and made certain the man and his children had a police escort all the way home to Kathmandu.

5

He Was With Me,
It Was Written on the Wall

by Rowan Clifford
(pseudonym used for security reasons)

"*S*it down there," the policeman ordered harshly, pointing to the wooden bench. "We will take you to a special police hotel and you can get your plane tomorrow."

"But you don't understand, I don't need a visa to get into Morocco!" I insisted in Arabic to the stone-faced Tunisian. "I want to leave now!"

I felt frustrated and angry. All my rights had been violated. The policeman turned away and went down the hall, into an office.

I did not like the way the man had said "special" hotel. I sat down on the wooden bench and leaned my head against the gray wall. Everything in the room was gray. Frustration tore at my mind. I hated being in police stations but this was worse — it was the Ministry of the Interior.

The day before, I had been escorted to a travel agent so I could pay for a ticket to Morocco. Why wouldn't they let me get on the plane? My passport showed I had already been in

27

that country without a visa. I was looking forward to getting back to Morocco. In my pride I could picture surprising the team with how I'd gotten kicked out of Tunisia. Unable to call them, they were unaware of my situation and didn't know I was supposed to fly in.

Tunisia, for me, had just meant hours and hours of police custody and interrogation. Being on the North Africa Travelling Team had its moments. Twice, my friends Rob and Chris, and myself, had been caught handing out Gospels of John. Once in a small country town we had spent twelve hours being interrogated by police because Rob was caught putting Bibles in a house's mail slot at 5:00 a.m. The surprised look on the Police Commissioner's face when he pulled out over a thousand books from our bags is something that would give me joy for a long time to come. He did not like the fact that we were handing out Scriptures that might turn people to Jesus Christ. To him, it was a crime.

Ironically, they had detained me this time when I went to the police station to pick up a visa extension that I had applied for a month before. Unfortunately, they knew my record. My passport was confiscated and they told me to come back in the morning with my bags. I was to be expelled from Tunisia and sent back to Morocco. During my pre-Christian life of crime I had never gotten into this much trouble with the police!

I wondered what this special police station would be like. *"Jesus"*, I prayed quietly to myself, *"please help me not to hate these people."* I looked up to see the policeman returning.

"Grab your bags," he commanded, "and get on the bus."

"But I want to get on the plane, I already paid for the ticket and don't want to miss my flight," I cried.

He looked at me like I was an insolent child. Moving around behind me he grabbed my belt and carried me like a piece of meat on a hook into a dirty white minibus. He sat practically on top of me, crushing me against the wall of the bus. His hands felt my right leg, noticing my artificial leg.

"What's this?" he said, more to himself.

"None of your business and don't touch me!" I told him, looking into his eyes. He backed off and I turned away to look out the window. I wanted to cry.

We came up the driveway of a large complex of buildings with a tall cement wall around it. The steel gate opened and we passed two guards armed with automatic weapons. Waves of horror gripped me as I realized this was no hotel, but a prison. I was marched out of the bus and into a small room connected to a courtyard with two larger buildings on either side, like grandstands of a tennis court. Walking by, I looked through the metal bars into the courtyard. Tall Central Africans were staring back out at me. Insane old men, unkempt and dressed in rags, wandered aimlessly about. I was petrified.

"Jesus, help me," I cried inside. In the guardroom, my bag was emptied and searched for sharp objects. Shouting erupted outside in the courtyard. Fighting had broken out between the Africans.

"Put him in," the guard ordered two men standing by.

Hurriedly they helped me repack my things. Ushering me out the door and through the courtyard, past a man who was now being subdued by the other guards, they took me into a long cell inside one of the larger buildings. I heard the clank of the metal door being locked behind me. I had no rights; I wasn't even allowed to call anyone. All I could think about immediately, though, were the dark faces of about twenty men, most of whom were Arab with a few Central Africans, staring at me. What were these people in here for? Some of the $600 U.S. I had in my pocket would have to be given to the biggest of these guys for protection, I thought. Anything could happen to me here. Terror filled my heart, as I realized no one knew where I was. The team in Tunis thought I was in Morocco, and in Morocco they thought I was still in Tunisia. God knew; I would have to trust in Him.

"Oh Australian, Australian!" someone called out. I looked toward the owner of the voice and recognized him from the Ministry of Interior building. He too had been accused of some crime. It was great to see a friendly face. I put my things down onto one of the dirty mattresses and sat down to talk with him. He was Moroccan and had tried to enter Italy illegally on a forged passport. The story was similar for most of them.

Before coming to Tunisia, I had spent six months in Morocco; so being locked up with Moroccans was as good as being locked up with some of my own countrymen. Getting to know them and sharing knowledge of their country eased my fears. There would be no need to pay protection money.

I crawled onto my mattress, prayed and read my Bible. The Psalms seemed the most appropriate reading and the words of Psalm 3 spoke to me like water to a thirsty man: *"Oh, Lord, how many are my foes! How many rise up against me!.... But you are a shield around me."* Night came slowly, and morning dawned even slower.

I awoke that next day with an inner energy. I had to make good use of the situation I was in. I wondered how God would use me in this place. After a breakfast of dry, tough bread with a little jam and some coffee in a bowl, I got into a discussion on religion with some of my cellmates. They were interested in what I believed and how an Australian came to be in a Tunisian jail. I later got out my Arabic/English New Testament and spent the rest of the day sharing the Gospel with my new-found friends. It was painstakingly hard as they were Muslims and believed in Mohammed as their prophet, even though they were criminals in jail. I tired myself out trying to tell them how Jesus died to save them from their sins. Even one of the guards, with his machine gun on his lap, listened in. We later spent many hours talking about Jesus. The constant speaking in Arabic drained me. By the afternoon I just wanted to spend some time on my own in the courtyard.

Sitting to one side on a step, I watched the mentally insane people walking around and thought how much worse their situation was than mine. Many of them needed medical treatment. Some argued with unseen foes, others dragged themselves around the dusty courtyard, struggling just to keep dressed. The youngest of them was my age; he just ran around in circles every time they let him out of his cell.

Looking up, I saw some of the guys I had been sharing the Gospel with approaching me. They stood me to my feet and asked if I wanted to become a Muslim. Before I had the chance to answer, a number of them surrounded me and began chanting the *Shahada* — the Muslim declaration of faith. The haunting Arabic incantation sent chills of fear through me. "There is no god but Allah and Mohammed is his sent one. There is no god but Allah...."

On and on they went. I was scared. I felt like I was at my weakest point. They were psychologically pushing me to the edge as they encircled me, trying to force me to become a Muslim. If they could only get me to repeat the Shahada, to them, I would be a Muslim. Fear and uncertainty shook me. What were they going to do to me?

Looking into the eyes of the men surrounding me I did not see love. I did not see God. I had never felt so alone. Where were my friends, where were my teammates? *"Oh Lord, give me peace,"* I thought. I just wanted to run, to cry out to the guards to let me out.

"You now have to learn Arabic well so you can become a Muslim," an inmate dressed in shorts with a cigarette in his mouth told me.

"How then can someone who does not know Arabic become a Muslim?" I asked shakily. "Does that mean those crazy people can't be Muslims?"

"Oh no, my friend! They are Muslims. Come, I'll show you." He took me by the hand and led me to the deranged young man who had been running in circles. Joined by the others, we all focused our attention on him. By now he was panting, looking up at us dazedly. "Who is your prophet?" the man asked him.

"Mohammed, the Japanese man," he replied innocently.

Spontaneously we all burst out laughing. The man with the cigarette was now trying to explain the question again to the disturbed youth. He looked rather annoyed. *"Jesus, thank you!"* was all I could think. The fear and stress washed off me.

After breakfast I brushed the dirt off my bed, laid down and read my Bible. I did not feel like reading my Bible at all. Why did God let me get imprisoned? Why was I here all by myself? The guard with whom I had shared the Gospel the day before came in and sat down beside me. I had given him the last of my Tunisian money in order to call the Australian Embassy in France, to let them know that I had been imprisoned. We talked. He had not been able to place the call and the money was used up. I was still stuck. No one had told me when I would be released. It could be weeks or months. How long would it take my team to realize I wasn't in Morocco or where I should be in Tunisia?

"I hate it here," I thought.

By the third evening my frustration had come to a head. I wanted to escape. Imprisonment wasn't like the hymn singing and angelic manifestations I read about in the Book of Acts. Sitting on a bed that was near the gray wall covered with graffiti, I pondered my situation.

Depression was enveloping me; yet I knew, strangely, that God was with me. He was by my side.

My eyes scanned the wall. Suddenly I was stunned to read the word *"Jesus"*. I couldn't believe what I was reading. Scrawled crudely on the wall in English were the words. *"Trust in the Lord Jesus and he will surely do it for you."* I kept staring at the letters — my heart lifting with an inexpressible joy.

Yes, God was with me here in this dingy cell! I knew it! He is so good. It was as though those words were written just for me. I was awed at how God had orchestrated the previous sufferings of a fellow brother in the Lord to encourage me in my greatest time of need.

I resolved to record this treasured moment and take a photo of the writing. The guards came into the cell as usual to check on us. With their automatic rifles slung over their shoulders they inspected the room and locked it on the way out. I watched them as they left, then quietly took out my camera and motioned some of my Moroccan friends over. I asked one of them to take the photo. Reluctantly he agreed and I sat between two others with the writing over my head. I prayed that it would turn out. After a warning from my fellow cellmates that taking pictures in prison is forbidden, I stuffed the camera deep into my bag. I felt really, really good.

The next day breakfast was even worse. The bread, I was sure, was older than I was. As we were standing around in the courtyard, the same white minibus drove up to the gate and some of the policemen from the Ministry of Interior got out. A flicker of hope leapt in my heart. Was I to be let out? Names were called. My name came and quickly I got my things together, almost forgetting to say goodbye to my friends. Halfway through the gate I turned around.

"Think about what we discussed," I yelled to the others, then left that dismal hospital/prison behind.

Back in the Ministry of Interior, I was led into the head of the department's office. He was a heavy-stomached man with a round face and a black bushy moustache. I was not even noticed as he talked with his minions that were hovering about his desk.

"Why did you put me in prison?" I finally demanded, bringing silence to the room.

"Because you distributed Christian literature," he answered angrily. He than named the towns I had visited with the travelling team. "Do you have money?"

"Yes, why?"

"You will be taken to the port and escorted onto the ferry to Italy. The ticket will be at your own expense." He motioned disdainfully to a subordinate to take me out of the room, as though I were a dog.

I was driven in style to the port in a brand new BMW, then escorted onto the boat. After I paid for a cabin the policeman left. I was free. Three days of frustration and tension rolled off me as I praised God for getting me out of prison. When I arrived on the shores of Italy, I quickly found a phone and rang my team leader in Morocco.

Later in the airport in Rome, waiting to fly back to Morocco, I thought about my time in prison. I hadn't been broken out of my cell by angels nor had I seen one of the prison guards and his family become Christians. No one from the team had even known where I was. I had learned something, though: that God is with us even when we don't feel Him. He is there in our darkest times. He is able to bring us through any situation.

Sometimes to see this we only need to open our eyes — it is as plain as writing on the wall.

6

Prisoners, and Yet...

*by Dave Bradley**
*(*Name changed for security reasons)*

*T*he interrogator sitting at the scarred wooden desk stroked the corners of his moustache like the arch-typal villain of a melodrama. He tried again, unconvincingly, to allay our fears. "Don't worry. Everything will be okay. Just sign these statements and I'll let you go."

Merv and I were just far enough away that he couldn't hear our muttered exchange. "I don't trust this guy any further than I can spit," I said. "He already told us not to worry several times. If there's nothing to worry about, then why are we still here after five hours of questioning?"

My Canadian companion and I had finished four weeks of backpacking in the Himalayan mountains of Nepal that autumn of 1988. I was a seasoned trekker, but on that 31st day when the Phidim police took us into custody and our belongings thoroughly searched, I had to wonder if it was the end of the trail for me.

The dark, arrogant eyes of the District Superintendent of Police narrowed. "You came here breaking the law with your propaganda. Why? Why did you come to Phidim? Answer all

35

the questions and you will be free to go home. Tell me. Where did you get these books?"

His air of self-importance was raising my hackles. "We've told you before. There is nothing illegal in our possession." Did he see through my bluff? I didn't need a stethoscope to hear my heart pounding a staccato beat on my eardrums. "You have held us against our will despite the fact that you've caught us doing nothing wrong. We only came to this town because it's the first place we could get a bus back to Kathmandu."

"Besides," interjected Merv, "you found our permits and passports in order. You've refused to let us talk to a lawyer, which is a violation of international law."

The DSP was finding it hard to follow our English. He turned to his translator and began gesturing toward our baggage. It didn't make any sense. Our porter's sack and rucksack had already been searched once. What were they looking for?

"Open the bags," he ordered one of his men. "Empty them. I want to see everything."

Sleeping bags, ponchos, two packets of granola, a large cooking pot and ladle, and several empty burlap sacks were soon strewn about the floor. The sacks had been full to the brim only a few days before. My qualms eased slightly, knowing that Christian books identical to those found in our shoulder bags during the first search would never be found.

"What's this?" The police chief, second-in-command, grabbed a couple of innocuous-looking cardboard squares and tore them apart, exposing two small records in paper sleeves. A knowing grin crept from ear to ear. My stomach knotted.

"Where is the gramophone?"

"What gramophone?"

"Where is the gramophone?" The chief's fat hands tore at the side pockets of our rucksacks and brought more records

into view. His grin widened. He continued searching: Tooth-brush, pocketknife, clothes... a handful of loose papers.

I groaned inwardly and rolled my eyes in self-disgust. "Oh no, Lord, don't let him see what's in those papers." Merv looked at me questioningly. "It's my journal. It tells everything about the trek — where we've been, who we met, how much literature was distributed. Everything."

Both of us stared at the papers but they refused to disappear.

"What is it?" demanded the superintendent in Nepali. The other officer shrugged. "It's written in English...." Delighted discovery suddenly stabbed the thick air. "It's a diary!" The translator read a few lines to them, and the two officers turned their gaze upon us. Neither one was smiling now.

Merv and I and three of our porters were placed in a custody cell, ten feet wide and ten feet long. It was the first day of what was to stretch into many long months of uncertainty.

After four days, everyone agreed the porters were not guilty of anything and they were finally released. We gave them money, a sleeping bag and cooking pot. Inside the sleeping bag was a note intended for Connie, my wife, telling her we needed a lawyer. At our first court appearance that day, the judge had indicated we could be liable for three years in prison. Six years was the sentence for successfully proselytizing (indicated by a convert's baptism). Three years was the standard sentence for anyone "attempting to proselytize," which could even mean preaching; and three years for "disturbing the Hindu community." Later the judge changed his estimate to between three to six years. I knew he had already made up his mind that we were guilty.

On Day 8, Merv and I were transferred to the main part of the prison. We found our own places on the floor and quickly made friends with five other men who gathered around and tried to teach us some Nepali. I made mistakes so they wouldn't realize that I knew the language. When I asked the friendliest of them why he was in prison he thumped his chest and declared, "I die a man," — meaning he had killed a man. Later we discovered that sixteen of our fellow inmates were charged with murder, eight with theft. We also began to learn about some of the punishments imposed upon these prisoners during police custody, before reaching prison. Leg irons or manacles attached to the wall were common. Many endured torture, strung up by the feet and beaten with rods on their feet and bodies. The police even stuck pins under their nails and shoved chili up their noses. One man who I had thought had always been retarded had only become that way after blows to the head. I was filled with outrage at such injustices, and at my inability to do anything about them.

We were allowed to roam the compound inside the high walls during the day. Near the end of the second week, while I was doing exercises, my foot slipped into a hole. The other inmates massaged it with hot oil but my ankle continued to give me pain. Only months later, after my release, did an x-ray show the ankle bone had been fractured.

Bed bugs also kept us awake many nights, and minor colds. The worst of our plight, however, was not knowing what was going on outside. We had been refused bail, and although we had sent a message to our embassies via the police in Kathmandu, we had no idea if it was delivered. It hurt to think of Connie and my son Jason —only five months old when I last saw him— trying to carry on without me. And how were my parents dealing with this, back in the States? I told myself that God knew how to care for my family better than I did.

Four weeks of imprisonment passed and we were shown court documents with fabricated statements by "witnesses," all saying we had sold books, records and tapes, and even preached. Strangely, all appeared to know my name as well. I was sure these people had been forced into writing what they did under fear of police retaliation.

Day 50: A friend arrived! South Asia Area Coordinator Mike Wakely had traveled all the way from England to the isolated mountains of Nepal to bring us news, food, and mail. Among the letters was a picture of Connie and Jason. It was a weird feeling not to recognize my son, he had changed so much in the almost three months since I'd seen him! Merv and I were tremendously encouraged by the messages from family and friends. Oh, the joy of being loved!

Three days later we received a surprise visit from the Consul of the U.S. Embassy. He told us the State Department had registered a complaint with the Nepal government for not notifying the embassy of their detention of an American citizen. The Consul said he hadn't known of our existence until a few days before, when Mike and two other friends visited him.

Day 73: We heard on the radio that drug barons had kidnapped two missionaries in Colombia. How insignificant our plight seemed in comparison to theirs! Those men stood a good chance of not coming out of their ordeal alive. In our confinement, Merv and I were able even to send and receive mail. We began to pray for those two missionaries. Psalm 69:33 would always hold new meaning for me: "God's prisoners are not despised."

Day 79: The dread of being separated for a long time from Connie and Jason was growing larger. I had begun to feel that I HAD to be released. Connie's letters reflected her struggles. Jason had been sick. My concern for them was overwhelming me. Could I surrender it to God? It hurt, it hurt! I wanted to be reunited with them. But I didn't want to sell out, either. That night Merv and I sang songs of praise. My heart was heavy, and I needed to lift it up to the Lord.

On January 18th, day 84, we had more visitors. My first anxious question was about Jason's condition. He was fine, these friends assured me. And it appeared that the news about our situation was spreading. The story had been aired on Canadian television and hit major newspapers coast to coast; my mother had been on TV in the States, and all Christian publications carried the report. Our visitors brought us a walkman and tapes, and even smuggled in some books in Nepali which were well received by the other inmates.

Our prison cell was getting crowded. In three months the population had grown from 28 to 43. The judge called us in again and told us he didn't like Christians and wanted to see all Christian organizations out of Nepal. Not encouraging.

Day 91: At last I was able to see Connie and Jason again, face to face! We held each other for a long time. Connie was definitely thinner in the face, but she looked good. Poor Jason was tired from the long trip. We were allowed only two hours together, but they planned to stay for eight or ten days and we were able to spend much of it together.

On January 26th we were back in court, this time for the cross-examination of witnesses. The Nepali lawyer we'd obtained seemed confident of our acquittal, but he still hadn't gotten a copy of my journal and thus didn't know all I'd written! The grim news was that we were up for a six-year sentence, not three. Only four out of the eleven witnesses appeared, and their statements were not consistent. One man even admitted that he had signed his name to the prepared statement only because the police told him to. That took courage. I prayed that God would bless him for it.

Saying goodbye to Connie and Jason was hard, although our week together did a lot to settle my fears for them. Connie was planning to return for our final hearing, set for February 28th. I sensed she was pessimistic about our release. Merv also had periods of depression. The district officer told us that the judge could make a decision on our case at the hearing. He asked if we would prefer to transfer to Kathmandu if we were convicted — a disconcerting question.

It was difficult to know how much was being done about our situation in official circles. Although we were now getting letters of support from 25 to 30 countries around the world and guessed there were thousands praying for us, this action was a result of the Christian network. The Canadian First Secretary came to visit on February 5th, the same day Merv suddenly got very sick. He had a terrible time breathing and the doctor had to be called. He thought it was bronchial asthma. The next day Merv was unable to eat. Proper health care was very far away, but we prayed, and quite soon, thankfully, his condition began to improve.

The week before our hearing we received a lot of encouragement from the other prisoners. Ser, who had been a friend from the start and would be spending the next ten years in jail, declared outright that he was a Christian now and nothing could make him change. I challenged another man, Mohan, who said he was going to follow the Lord when he got out. A big surprise came when someone from outside the prison came and asked me for a Christian book. I sensed that God was bringing things to a head. Merv and I also believed that God had done something good inside us through these months of imprisonment.

On the afternoon of February 27th, our friend Mike, the U.S. Embassy Consul and an assistant, the Canadian Consular Officer, plus an American reporter arrived in Phidim. Connie couldn't come, but she had written. She said she feared that we would not get released, and Merv's mother felt the same. That hit us hard. From other letters we knew that this was a day of fasting and prayer throughout the OM world. In the evening Merv and I committed ourselves to God and had what we hoped would be our last communion service in prison. Since we had no bread or crackers, we substituted chocolate!

February 28th: Merv and I packed up all of our belongings in case we were set free. The time passed slowly until 10 a.m. when we were finally called to go to court. The judge asked to see us in his office.

"What do you want today?" he asked. Merv replied, "We want what God wants." The judge didn't like that answer. I spoke up and said we wanted to be found not guilty, and he dismissed us.

Our lawyer had convinced the judge to allow the curious local people outside to hang in the windows and crowd into the courtroom. After the judge convened the trial the court lawyer gave an inspirited, five-minute argument on why we should be given a six-year sentence. Our Nepali lawyer then spoke for over an hour, explaining why we should be set free. His appearance and presentation were impressive. At one point this unsaved man took a school textbook of world religions and read several pages about Jesus! Quite a few nodded their heads in agreement when the lawyer pointed out that this was a government-sanctioned book, and if we were sentenced for our books than so must every teacher in Nepal! The judge agreed with this argument. We were given a two-hour recess, then he returned with the verdict. Not guilty! MERV AND I WERE ACQUITTED!

The legal proceedings were completed and we returned to the prison, only to find our belongings had already been placed outside. We were not allowed inside to say goodbye to anyone, which made us sad. We stood at the small door and spoke to Ser and the rest of our friends as well as we could.

Disturbed by rumors that Merv and I would be taken into Kathmandu under police escort, our friends urged us to hurry out of Phidim. We carried our bags to a jeep parked on a hill overlooking the prison. When that was done I shouted down to the inmates: "JESUKO JAI!" - "Victory to Jesus!". They responded, "JAI!" - "Praise to the Lord!"

We piled into the jeeps. Twisting and turning up the mountain we could look far below to the prison from which Merv and I had so often looked up, tracing the route to freedom. Now, at last, we were on that road. Nepal would never again be the same for us. And we ourselves would never be the same.

7

"I'm in Your Hands!"

*J*onathan and Trevor were stretched out in the back of the car, fast asleep. Pedro felt as though he'd been driving the long road from Portugal to Barcelona, Spain, forever. He never knew the exact moment his tired eyes closed, his fatigued body slumped at the wheel. Nor was he aware of what was happening when the car shot straight across the highway into the path of an oncoming truck.

Those who first arrived at the scene of that 1982 accident thought it was all over for Pedro. The young man from Barcelona sat unmoving, groaning with pain. But although Pedro and Trevor would always bear the scars of that accident, their injuries proved relatively minor. It was Jonathan McRostie's body that suffered the worst impact. Jonathan's spinal cord was severed, leaving him paralyzed from mid-chest downwards. OM's European Coordinator would never walk again.

A week after the accident, Jonathan was flown by hospital plane to the Brussels Center of Traumatology and Readaptation. He spent the next six weeks in traction and another month in a "Striker" frame. After three months of continuous therapy, he was able to sit in a wheelchair. "A day at a time" was the motto that he and his wife, Margit, and three children learned to adopt through the next long months of rehabilitation.

43

On the eve of being discharged from the center, Jonathan wrote: "I have served the Lord with Operation Mobilization for twenty years in Europe. For just over a year, I have lived in a hospital as a tetraplegic.... On April 14, 1982 our car hit a truck. When I woke and realized my legs couldn't move, I prayed: "Will I die? No, I don't think so. Lord, I want my heart right. Forgive even the thought of sins yesterday. I'm in your hands."

"Since that moment, God graciously gave His peace and has not withdrawn it despite the most unusual year of my life."

"A Christian handicapped or a Christian dedicated to helping the handicapped can only ultimately 'succeed' by confident dependence on God and faithful obedience to Him. Physically my head gives the right instructions but my lower body hears not, obeys not, for the cord is severed. Spiritually, we must have a spinal cord of faith and obedience connecting us with our Creator and Savior-Lord. There's only one way to go for the Christian —FORWARD!— even if it's with faltering steps and frequent falls. *With God we can do it.*"

From the beginning Jonathan refused to be sidelined. He soon resumed business correspondence, continued to advise OM as European Coordinator, and even occasionally preached. During the more than fifteen years since his accident he has traveled through over 80 airports in 35 countries and inspiring countless audiences to a greater involvement in missions. In addition to his present role as minister-at-large with OM, Jonathan is International Chairman of OM World Partners, a fellowship of former OMers. He also serves as an advisor to Joni & Friends (JAF) Ministries, Europe. Joni's contact with Jonathan began shortly after his accident and he has now undertaken to promote JAF's goals of handicap awareness, accessibility and ministry in Europe's churches.

Spain retains a special place in Jonathan McRostie's heart. Many years before his accident, he and Margit spent their honeymoon there. Ten years after the accident he was honored to act as a chaplain at the 1992 Paralympics in Spain.

Why does God allow death or severe injury to men and women engaged in His work? Jonathan reflects: "We all have such questions, and we don't always receive full explanations. God has not promised them. But He does assure us, 'I am with you. I understand all you are going through. And I am in control.' Therefore we can trust and faithfully serve Him!"

HIS
PROTECTIVE
TOUCH

8

Helping Hands

It was 1982 and American Robert Suhonen was discovering the land of his roots, Finland. He and his travelling companion, Brian, had never before been so far north. In fact, finding themselves next door to Russia, it seemed too good an opportunity to miss. The two entrepreneurs came up with a fantastic moneymaking scheme. They would buy up all the jeans they could afford, sell them across the border, and buy furs with the profits.

Gradually, however, feelings of guilt began to set in. As Christians, shouldn't they be more focused on getting God's good news into Russia than making money? Robert and Brian decided they would smuggle in Christian literature instead.

The pair joined a tour group going into Russia. They knew little about the ways and means of transporting forbidden literature, so they elected to tape it to their bodies. The group arrived at the border. The Finns got through with no problem, but the two Americans were singled out for interrogation.

"Their machine guns were pointed right at me!" remembers Robert. "I kept saying in my spirit, *'in the name of Jesus, they can't find this literature!'* — but in my body I was a nervous wreck. The guard went through my pockets. Then he started frisking me. He didn't miss an inch. I remember so clearly praying, *'Lord, into your hands I commit my spirit!'*

"He pressed those books right into me. And then, unbelievably, he said, *'You can go!'*

"When I remember that day I still can't believe we did it. We didn't know anything, couldn't speak a word of Russian. But that was the day God called me to Eastern Europe.

"We didn't even know what to do with the literature once we made it through! We got lost in the city, walked up and down the streets. Finally we felt God wanted us to leave it at a certain door. Later, we learned it was exactly the right place."

9

Rescue!

by Chacko Thomas,
as told to Anne Buchanan Kammies

G et out of here! These are all lies! You are trying to bring the British back to India!"

Even in the 1960's and 1970's, few people living in the scattered villages of the North Indian countryside had ever heard the good news of Christ. OM teams set out every day on foot, on bicycles and in trucks to cover as much territory as they could.

One day during the summer of 1972, a team led by Chacko Thomas decided to visit a huge fresh produce market. The market was a weekly event that attracted thousands of men and women from surrounding villages. As soon as their truck arrived, the men swung into action, lowering the tailboard to use as a platform and attaching a loudspeaker to the roof. The team soon gathered a crowd with their singing. Chacko gave a series of short messages, and between each one, the men sold New Testaments and other Christian books. The most popular offer was an inexpensive packet consisting of Billy Graham's *"How to Find God"*, two Gospels, plus three other booklets. The team was thrilled to sell about 500 of these packets. The day was going much better than expected.

As evening approached, however, an angry young man suddenly appeared by the truck. He started shouting at the team members, accusing them of spreading false propaganda and poisoning people's minds. Within minutes he turned the happy crowd into a dangerous, seething mob.

Chacko wisely decided it was time to leave. Three of the team had wandered away from the truck, but he couldn't pause to look for them. Nine men piled into the back and with Chacko and the driver in front, they slowly maneuvered their 7-ton truck out of the field and onto a narrow mud track, heading for the main road. A short way down the track, however, a hastily erected roadblock halted them. There they sat, surrounded by a violent sea of Hindus and Muslims.

A few men started picking up clods of sunbaked mud from the nearby field. Soon the rock-hard missiles were being hurled at the windshield. When these failed to break the glass, the crowd moved around to the driver's side and began pulling on the closed window, trying to slide it down. After a while they succeeded in opening it enough to slap the English driver's face. Eventually they managed to open the door and pull him down into a ditch. There they began to beat him.

Chacko opened his side of the truck and jumped down, drawing the attention of the mob towards himself. Those who were nearest shoved him against the bank of the ditch, tore his shirt, and struck him with their shoes — an act considered of great offense in the Indian culture. The attackers then proceeded to rain punches all over his body.

Nine team members were still safely hidden in the back of the closed truck. They prayed fervently, knowing that darkness was falling, and no other towns were nearby. The possibility of rescue seemed remote.

Just at that moment, however, a jeep suddenly appeared at the blockade, pulling up next to the truck. A jeep was a symbol of great status in this isolated area of the world where most people used bullock carts. The three passengers were Indian in appearance. In contrast to the loincloths and turbans worn by most of the crowd, however, they were dressed in formal black suits. The people melted fearfully away.

The three men got out of their jeep and pulled Chacko and the driver from the ditch. Chacko told them about the team members who had been left behind in the market, but his rescuers advised him not to wait. They must get back in the truck and leave at once. As the truck pulled away, the jeep followed closely. Once they were clear of the crowds the jeep increased its speed and left the heavy truck far behind.

The team was still worrying about their missing men and wondering what to do when, to their utter astonishment, they saw their friends standing on the roadside in front of them! The truck halted, and the three men eagerly told their story. They, too, had been attacked in the market, they explained, and had been forced to look on helplessly while all their books were torn to shreds. Just as this was going on, a large man had suddenly pushed through the frenzied throng. After reaching the team members, he escorted them safely to the edge of the market. He had then instructed them to walk up the road and wait for the truck.

The team had a lot to rejoice about that night. They were all safe. Chacko and the driver had not been seriously injured, and quantities of literature had gone out to people who needed the liberating news of Christ. Most wonderful of all, they were witnesses to the faithfulness of the Master when there was no way out — but up.

10

Walking Through the Night

by Carey Hauri

I stepped off the bus and began to trudge up the hill, pulling my coat tighter about me to keep out the chilly Hungarian night air. My steps were laborious; every movement was restricted by the chiropractic back brace strapped around my torso. I hated wearing it but knew that I should obey doctor's orders.

I could hear someone walking behind me. Probably just someone else on his way home, I thought. I finally got to the top of the stairway and started walking along the main street, which led the rest of the way up the hill. I could still hear the footsteps behind me. They were speeding up and getting closer, which didn't surprise me. My back brace really slowed me down.

Then, suddenly, someone grabbed me from behind. An arm gripped me tightly around my neck. I struggled to free myself but couldn't. I craned my head around to try and catch a glimpse of my attacker. It was dark, so I couldn't see much except the shadowy outline of a man, shorter than I but stronger, with dark hair. The man mumbled a few words in Hungarian, which I couldn't understand. I didn't know what to do. *"This is it,"* I thought, *"my life is over."*

I screamed and screamed, hoping that maybe someone would hear me and come to help. I couldn't think of anything else to say or do. My mind was so numb that I couldn't even think to pray and cry out to God. The limited Hungarian I knew completely deserted me. I was totally incapable of coherent thought. I grabbed the arm that was around my neck and tried to pry it loose but the man continued to grip me tightly. My legs buckled and I found myself kneeling on the road. With my raised right arm I instinctively shielded my face. I felt something press hard into my back.

At that moment my brain started working again. *"I think I'm being stabbed,"* I thought to myself, surprised by such remarkable objectivity and logic. I waited for the pain but strangely enough, didn't feel any. All I could feel was something digging into my back. I continued to scream as I knelt helplessly in the dirt. Then, unexpectedly, my attacker loosened his grip and I heard the sound of running feet. I turned around in time to see his shadowy figure race off down a dark, narrow lane leading back down the hill.

I staggered to my feet. My hand felt wet. I stared at it, dripping with blood. I started to cry. My other hand was fine so I used it to hold my back in a vain attempt to staunch the blood that I expected was flowing from there also. Slowly, I walked up the hill, sobbing uncontrollably. If I could just make it home!

It was at that moment that I awoke. *"Thank God!"* I breathed in relief. It was only a bad dream.

I tried to turn over and go back to sleep but a sharp pain jolted me wide-awake. Something was digging into my back. Gingerly I reached behind me and my fingers found a plastic tube dangling over the side of the bed.

"What's that doing there?" I wondered groggily. Then it hit me: I hadn't been dreaming after all. I looked around the room. A hospital ward. How had I gotten there? Then I remembered.

I had only gone a few steps up the hill when a young couple had come running towards me. They must have heard my screams. They asked if I was okay and gently helped me walk to a small bar half way up the hill. I'd passed the place many times but had never ventured inside. As we entered people immediately flocked around me, clucking with concern. The barmaid took a cloth and wrapped it around my bleeding hand. It stung but looked worse than it actually was. I pointed at my back but no one could see anything wrong with it.

I removed my jacket. Everyone gasped when they saw the huge patch of blood that had seeped through the several layers of clothing I was wearing. Someone rang the police and the ambulance. Several men raced from the bar to find my attacker, but I was sure they'd never catch him. It was too easy to disappear in the tangle of streets and lanes that crisscrossed the hill. By the time the ambulance arrived I'd calmed down enough to realize that I wasn't going to die just yet, after all.

It was a bumpy ride to the hospital. I gripped the metal rail bordering the stretcher with my fingers and toes so that I wouldn't slide around too much or bounce off the mattress altogether. After arrival I was wheeled around on a stretcher and examined by a number of doctors, including a neurosurgeon who spoke excellent English. They all shook their heads in disbelief when they heard what had happened and promptly blamed the new western influences flooding the country.

Someone stitched and dressed the stab wound in my back: a horizontal gash three centimeters long and two centimeters deep. A tube was inserted to drain the blood from the wound.

"You're lucky," the neurosurgeon said. "A few millimeters either way and the knife could have hit your spinal cord or punctured your lung."

"I'm not 'lucky'," I told him, "God was looking after me!"

The doctor thought for a moment. "That doesn't make sense. If God was looking after you, why did he let this happen to you in the first place? He wasn't looking after you very well, was He?"

I thought about that, and remembered my back brace. What would have happened if I hadn't been wearing it? The knife had actually glanced off the top edge of the brace, so wearing it had spared me the full force of the blow. My hated brace had actually acted as a life-saving shield.

"Yes," I finally answered the doctor. "God was definitely looking after me. I don't understand why this has happened, but it could have been a lot worse."

As I lay there the conversation came back to me. *"I don't understand, Lord,"* I thought. *"You saved my life by making sure I was wearing my back brace when I was attacked, but why did you even let it happen at all? Why did you let that man attack me? Do you really care about me?"*

My faith in the Lord was strong enough to ask questions and not be afraid of the answers. I tried to sleep but the questions continued to echo inside my head, demanding answers that didn't come. I felt very alone.

Gradually I saw that I had a choice to make. I could blame God for allowing the incident to happen —didn't I have a right to be angry with Him? At the same time, I also realized that if I took that road, I could end up by becoming a very bitter and disillusioned person, my relationship with the Lord being reduced to tatters.

My other option was to simply accept what had happened and trust that God had allowed it for reasons that maybe I would never understand. My faith would be severely tested but if it was as real and solid as I believed it to be, shouldn't it also be strong enough to get me through this? What good is faith if it can't carry me through the tough times? It's one thing to trust in God when life is good but doesn't the true test of faith come through the hard times?

I knew that for me there was only one way to go. I'd been in difficult situations before and God had never let me down. How could I turn away from Him now? If anything, now more than ever, I needed God in a special way. The thought of getting through this terrible ordeal on my own, without Him, was a worse nightmare than the one I had just experienced.

"OK, God, I don't understand why this has happened. But I'm going to keep believing in You anyway, and trust that You will somehow use this for good," I prayed at some time in the early hours of the morning. *"Help me to learn whatever it is that You want to teach me through this."*

A deep peace came over me and I sensed the presence of Jesus in a way I had never experienced before. It was as if He was sitting on the bed beside me. I fell asleep, secure in the knowledge that I really wasn't alone.

Two weeks later I was back at work. Although it took awhile for me to recover completely. I surprised others and myself at how I came through the experience relatively un-scathed.

Despite a physical scar to remind me that the attack had actually happened, the incident didn't seem to leave any long term psychological scars. For awhile I was afraid to go out at night on my own and at first, even during the day, I would become uneasy when people walked behind me. As the weeks and months passed, those fears slowly dissipated. In the hospital I had read Romans 8:35-39 a lot and those precious verses were my strength. *Nothing* could separate me from the love of Christ! Paul even mentioned a "sword". As far as I was concerned a knife was close enough. I was comforted by the fact that God had my situation covered!

Even today, I still don't understand why God allowed this attack, and possibly never will. But that's no longer the main issue for me. What's important to me is that my faith was tested, and it withstood the test. God didn't let me down.

11

The Touch of Safety

by Rex Worth

*G*od looks after us physically. One day when I was working as an engineer on *Logos,* I was using the lathe. Back then we weren't very safety conscious. I wasn't wearing goggles and got a bit of steel in my eye. Engineers don't take much notice of such things but this steel got rusty.

We had a wonderful doctor on board at the time, a Dr. Schmidt. She took one look at me and said there was nothing she could do. So we went into port there in Ethiopia, and she put me and another fellow into a van and sent us into the desert to a tiny village with only mud huts and a mission hospital. The fellow in charge of the hospital happened to be an American eye surgeon. He operated and dug out the steel as well as he could. But he told me I would have a scar and a blind spot for the rest of my life.

That was no big problem for me. But in the years since then, every time I've gone to the optician for a check-up I've asked him, *"Can you see a scar?"* And he says, *"No."* I've never had a scar — never had a blind spot. That's how God looks after you.

❖ ❖ ❖

On the *Logos* our book exhibition was up on the main deck. One day we had the hatch covers loose. The floor of the deck below was taken up, but halfway down the ship the beams were still in place. From the top of the hatch on the main deck to the bottom of the ship was a good fifty feet. One man working in the book exhibition fell through the hatch covers, missed the beams and fell all the way to the bottom. When we got down to the hold we were sure we would have to pick a body up. But all the man had was a broken wrist!

❖   ❖   ❖

Another seaman was taking part in a boat drill on the *Doulos.* When he started to climb down the rope ladder to the lifeboat, the shackle holding the ladder suddenly came out. The man fell from the deck of the *Doulos* all the way down to the lifeboat on the water. The force of the fall smashed the seat and he landed on his back. His wife was watching —she was the nurse. She thought her husband would never walk again. But he only had bruises. He got up and walked away.

❖   ❖   ❖

I honestly believe we have guardian angels that look specifically after the children on the ships. They've never had a major accident. I'll never forget the day at sea when one little girl got out of the nursery, climbed under the railings and under the lifeboat. Only a 2" sill separated her from the deep blue. She froze —couldn't shout, couldn't move. Somebody was finally able to coax her out to safety.

❖   ❖   ❖

We were working one day on the well deck. An electrician was trying to fix a fan and had it in pieces with the cover off. He went to switch the fan on to test the motor and just at that moment a little boy came along. He stuck his hand in. I expected him to come out without a hand, to be honest. But the fan started up and just blew his hand away. The boy laughed and went on to play.

12

Thanks to My Father

by Stephen Hart

ƥack in the Sixties when OM first pioneered the work in Turkey, there were a grand total of five known believers in the whole country. In Istanbul the team met a young man named Kenan Araz. Kenan was originally from a small town in the Far East, but he was studying in the city. Through this team he placed his faith in Jesus and became a radiant witness in that intensely Muslim nation.

Several years later, the police caught Kenan in the capital city of Ankara with a quantity of Christian literature. The distribution of non-Muslim material was and still is a highly inflammatory offence in Turkey. Kenan was promptly hauled into court. He knew the consequences could be severe.

Kenan's case was assigned at random to one of the court's one hundred judges. This judge studied the paper detailing the charges while Kenan stood before him.

"Hummm... *Araz*, eh? From Midyat?" He peered intently at the prisoner. Kenan was surprised that the judge had even heard of his little town, some six hundred miles away. But the judge's next question staggered him.

"Do you know an Enver Araz?"

63

"Yes, Sir. He's my father!"

The judge jumped up and went around the desk, embraced Kenan, and kissed him on both cheeks. "When you were studying in Istanbul," he said, "I was stationed in Midyat. Your father was one of my best friends. I was often in your home. *Tonight you shall be in mine!*"

The charges were dismissed.

13

"In All Your Ways..."

by Frank Dietz

We had stopped in a little village called Huriyer in the Indian State of Mysore to get a bite of lunch. Some of the fifteen Indian men on the team handed out gospel tracts as they walked toward the restaurant. While we were eating our rice and dahl we noticed a crowd was beginning to gather.

At first I thought people only wanted to look at my wife, Anneli. Blonde hair and blue eyes were something of a phenomenon in parts of India. We had only been married about two months, and in some ways we were still on our honeymoon.

But subtly the atmosphere in the restaurant changed. Fanatical Hindus were crowding in and a very real sense of animosity prevailed. We decided to leave quickly. After paying our bill we went outside and found several hundred Hindus surrounding our five-ton truck, in the act of letting the air out of the tires. Their intentions were obvious. We had almost four tons of Christian literature with us. They would immobilize our vehicle, then burn it.

My first concern was for my wife. I was able to get her into the cab of the truck and the driver — an Englishman and the only other Westerner with us — quickly got us underway. On other occasions when we ran into difficulty, we had always been able to shake off the opposition by the time we reached the village outskirts. But this time the Hindus chased us. They started with a truck; then, when they found they couldn't pass us, they switched to an ambassador car. They kept after us for thirty miles, putting up four different roadblocks. The last barrier was the most dangerous. They had gone ahead to another village and convinced the people there that we were kidnapping some Hindu children. Of course, when they saw young Indian team members among us, this seemed to confirm their story.

At the entrance to the village they had staggered three bullock carts across the road so that when we approached we would have to slow down and go around them. Village people were lined up on both sides, with rocks in their hands. By that time most of the windows of our vehicle, including the windshield, were already broken by previous rocks. The rear tires were in poor condition and likely to blow at any moment. To be honest, it looked to me like the end of the road.

Surprisingly, however, we made it through the gauntlet. Some of the rocks had found their mark, but our adrenaline was pumping and it made us — for the moment, at least — oblivious to pain. Half a mile on the other side of the village one of the bad rear tires exploded. We still had one on that side so we decided to keep on going to the next big city. The car that had been chasing us began to follow, but for some inexplicable reason it stopped. We found out later that it had run out of gas.

Just as we pulled into the city limits of Bellary, the remaining tire on the left side finally collapsed. Our vehicle wasn't going any further and we felt shaken, physically and emotionally. Since we obviously couldn't reach our intended destination, we contacted a small Methodist church in Bellary. With their help and the permission of a high caste Hindu, we set up some tube lights and loud speakers in his field near the city center and started preaching. In India it's very easy to gather a crowd!

Unfortunately, a nominal Christian in town decided to try to sabotage our efforts. The first night went well until the Indian evangelist with us started giving an invitation for listeners to accept Jesus Christ. At that point a Muslim magician, hired by our opponent, began making noise and distracting the crowd. When the same thing happened the second night, I jumped off the platform and confronted him. An Indian brother translated and told him that we were doing God's work. If he continued to interrupt God's work, he could expect God's judgment.

The next day about 3:00 o'clock, a strong wind began to blow. The storm was unusual in its ferocity, tearing down trees and interrupting the power system. The magician's tent, pitched near us, was completely demolished. When we passed by the next morning, he was cowering in the spot where his tent used to be, trembling with genuine fear. He approached one of the team. *"Who is your God?"* he demanded. In the next days one hundred people invited Christ into their lives.

But the story isn't quite over. Hundreds of miles north, OM's international coordinator George Verwer had come upon two Canadians touring India in a Land Rover. The pair had been planning to drive back to Great Britain, sell the vehicle, and use the money to fly home. The outbreak of a cholera epidemic in Pakistan, however, closed the border to Iran and squashed their plans. When George offered to buy the Land Rover at the price of two air tickets to Canada, they readily accepted.

George didn't really have a use for that vehicle, so he decided to send it down to me. He didn't know anything at that time of what we had just gone through. But in the midst of seeing God move in the city of Bellary, we woke up one morning to discover two Indian brothers rolling into the compound with our new vehicle. Needless to say, our hearts overflowed with gratefulness. God's provision, his intervention and his timing are always perfect!

14

Under Fire

*O*M South Africa sent its first team into Mozambique in 1990, knowing they would be facing tough conditions. Fifteen years of a war that was still going on had demolished the country's agricultural support system. This meant no food, no work and no money. Medical aid was nonexistent. Children's sores were treated with battery acid; other people walked around with cancer, gangrene, malaria and bilharzia. The team planned to focus on medical aid and building projects, children's evangelism and discipleship of believers.

The OM-ers traveled roads that were heavily patrolled by armed soldiers. Vehicles, shot to pieces and burnt out, littered the roadside. Most locals habitually carried weapons and hand grenades.

One night two opposing rebel forces opened fire near the place where the team had set up camp. "We had never lain so close to mother earth or prayed so desperately, realizing that any bullet could mean our final breath." Eight civilians were killed that night, and hundreds of houses burnt, destroying the little that people had left.

The day after the attack, a lady who lived across from us had this story to tell:

69

"I saw three heavily armed rebel soldiers coming down the road, heading straight for your camp. Just as they were entering the gate they suddenly stopped. Their faces displayed total shock, as if they'd had the fright of their lives. They turned around and ran as quickly as their legs could carry them!"

What sight had kept the rebels from their purpose? The team would never know. But they could go on with their work after that, filled with a comforting sense of being surrounded by unseen forces.

15

Typhoon!

by Debbie Meroff

I was just one among a shipload of seasick mariners who thanked God for reaching Japan's shores safely that August of 1996. The *MV Doulos* had cast off from her previous port of Shanghai a day early, after our captain became aware of a dangerously advancing typhoon. The pilot who was to guide us down the Huangpu and Yangtze Rivers told him he was afraid the tide was not full enough. If the *Doulos* had sailed only a half-hour later, he would have been right. Our ship would have been forced to anchor for another twelve hours. And the next day we would have run directly into mega-typhoon Herb.

Even so, our 300-plus staff and crew were warned to expect heavy weather. Vehicles and equipment on deck were securely lashed and personal items were safely stowed. As the 180-mph storm ran in back of the ship toward Taiwan, most of us were remembering the other occasions that summer when God had protected us. While we were tied up in Subic Bay, Philippines, we were stunned by the news that a typhoon was on its way toward Naha, Japan — exactly where our ship would have been if we had not had an unexpected cancellation. And on the way to Shanghai, the *Doulos* had just managed to run ahead of another violent typhoon called Gloria. Although "Herb" kicked up sizable seas, and few of us cared to swallow anything beyond bread and seasick tablets on the memorable passage to Japan, everyone was aware of how much worse it could have been.

But just as the *Doulos* came into calm seas outside Kagoshima harbor on the morning of August 2nd, the engine quit. A turbo charger had suddenly malfunctioned. The captain was forced to call tugboats to tow the *Doulos* to her berth.

A few days later on August 5th, Captain Graeme Bird and his staff began tracking another typhoon that seemed to be heading in our direction. Typhoon Kirk's behavior was worrying, revealing itself to be both erratic and powerful. In the next few days, the storm succeeded in putting one vessel aground and sinking another, its 22 passengers forced to abandon ship.

On Monday, the 12th of August, there was no longer any doubt the typhoon was headed directly for Kagoshima. The port authority ordered all vessels to clear the harbor. Ships that could make a run for it or ride at anchor normally had a good chance of escaping major damage. But the *Doulos* had no options. The replacement part for our engine hadn't arrived yet. We could only brace ourselves and pray for the best.

Deck and engine crewmen, forewarned, had already been working hard, laying on extra mooring lines and lashing down every movable object fore and aft with steel wires. Nothing, however, had prepared me for the horror of suddenly being jerked out of my sleep at about 3 a.m. on August 13th, when the full fury of Typhoon Kirk slammed into the *Doulos*. Fighting the ship's violent list to starboard I staggered to my feet and dressed quickly. Then I headed toward my office, anxious to check the safety of my computer. On the way I ran into a dozen deckmen in orange slickers. The expression on their faces didn't reassure me.

Once back in my cabin, I lay down on my bunk, fully dressed, reliving a rush of memories that threatened to swamp me with fear. I had been aboard the old *Logos* back in 1988 when she was shipwrecked off South America. Though it was long ago, I could still remember every detail of that January night —the shock, the fear, and the enormous sense of loss. A few years later I had sailed to South America again with the *Logos II.* In one port we were hit by a disastrous storm, and although we had come out of it without major damage, we had seen ships sunk all around us. People had lost their lives. I was aware now of what could happen in violent storms, even to ships as large as the *Doulos,* when they were tied up and helpless.

At around 4:00 a.m., I heard someone knocking on the cabin doors in my section. I recognized First Officer Steve Wallace's voice, advising cabin occupants to get up and dressed. Families, he added quietly, might want to prepare an emergency kit —just in case it should become necessary to evacuate the ship.

That did it. I had a horrifying sense of *deja vû,* as though the nightmares of the past had all come upon me once again. Panic seized me. I flung open my cabin door and Steve Wallace saw my face.

"We're all right, Debbie! Nothing is going to happen to us."

"That's what they said before!" I wailed. I couldn't seem to control my voice or the tears that slipped down my face. "It's just like what happened before! We could sink right where we are."

"We won't! Listen to me. I know this ship. I've checked everything out. Trust me, OK?"

I respected Steve's long sea experience. I knew I could trust his assessment. I nodded, unable to speak.

While waiting for the winds to spend themselves, I drew comfort from the Psalms. My *Daily Bread* devotional thought for that day also held a particularly relevant assurance: *"God does not keep us from life's storms, He walks with us through them."* I was learning something through Typhoon Kirk.

When Captain Bird called the crew together later that day, he confided that his greatest fear had been that one of the several large barges anchored near us might break loose and drive into our hull. This would have meant immediate evacuation at the worst of the storm.

Winds had reached up to 220 kph or Force 13 or 14 — "off the scale." But fortunately for the *Doulos,* the edge of the typhoon's eye did not hit broadside but astern on the port side, pushing the ship against the quay. Gusts caused a sharp list to starboard from 10 degrees all the way to 15. Unsecured articles went flying. Rain and seawater was driven through doors and porthole hatches, flooding starboard decks and cabins. Overflowing sewage lines also backed into some of the accommodation areas. Damages to books and equipment amounted to approximately $7,000.

"But we had the right berth," asserted the captain. "The wind came astern, and at any other berth we would have been blown off, losing the mooring lines. We did worry about lines washing off from the high waves. That would have been a problem. We were also concerned about the fender (protecting the hull from damage against the quayside). But it lasted through the storm, and only broke off at the end. By God's providence it was there as long as we needed it!"

The captain also made us dramatically aware of God's intervention in another way. He stated, "If we had gotten the engine part we needed, we would have had to sail. We couldn't have anchored — our anchor cable isn't long enough for the deep water here. So we just had to make all the preparations we could. —And they had to work!"

Of course, some would simply call it a piece of luck that the *Doulos* managed to evade at least three typhoons; and that our engine gave out only when we reached the harbor outside Kagoshima. They would also claim it was coincidence that a missing turbo charger had kept us in port during Typhoon Kirk, when three large ships, which did go to anchor, went aground. But don't try to convince any of us who were aboard God's ship *Doulos* that summer of 1996! —*We know better!*

16

Out of Control!

by Peter Dance

*I*n the early days of OM we tried to save money by transporting teams — even over vast distances — with our own vehicles. Changing border regulations and other factors have now made this impractical, but back then I drove overland from Europe to points East several times. Each trip was different, and the Lord taught me something new each time. But I think if I had to choose one trip that made a difference to my life in the most profound way, it was the first one.

I'd been a Christian only a short time — about a year and a half — when someone told me about Operation Mobilization's summer program and suggested I join. I was a mechanic by trade and had driven a truck all over England, so it made sense to me to link up with the Zaventem, Belgium, team as a mechanic. I grew in my faith and learned so much that summer that I decided to stay on another year.

That autumn, OM's ship *Logos* was expecting to visit the Persian Gulf. As usual there would be an exchange of crew members, and vehicles from Europe would be taking people and supplies out to the ship. They needed drivers. Since I was both an experienced driver and mechanic, they asked if I'd be willing. I thought it sounded exciting. I was in my mid-20's and confident that I was the ideal man for the job!

We prepared and serviced all the vehicles that would be travelling around the start of October. Of course, we first had to see a considerable amount of money come in. That meant some exciting times of worship and prayer as we witnessed God's power to meet our needs.

Altogether, we formed a convoy of eight or nine transit vans and trucks. Some of them were going to India, and some to the port in Iran where the ship was scheduled to arrive. Greg Livingston (later to become the founder of Frontiers Mission) and his family were the leaders of the convoy. We left in different groups, at intervals of a few days. I was called "tail-end Charlie" because I was the mechanic driving the large truck in the last group in case anyone broke down in front of us. The idea was to keep together as much as possible.

If I'd known everything we were heading into, I probably wouldn't have gone. Little did we imagine that we wouldn't be back in Belgium until the beginning of January, almost three months later.

I was to find that going through new countries was exciting, but not nearly as exciting as what I would learn from the Lord. In Turkey we stayed a few nights in the home of a Turkish believer. His gentleness, serenity, the close walk he had with the Lord was obviously very deep and real. His "where the rubber hits the road" kind of faith was a great challenge to me — a challenge that's stuck with me ever since.

Crossing eastern Turkey offered no problems. Then we came to Iran — my first border experience — and the authorities kept us a few days, inspecting every cubbyhole. When we reached our destination, Bandar 'Abbas, we heard the ship had been turned back from the port for a technicality and we had to wait another ten days until it was allowed in. At last, however, we were able to collect the crew members that were leaving the ship, and started back.

A thousand miles stretched ahead of us to Teheran. I drove the first few hundred miles through desert with miles of nothing in every direction. The roadway was laid several feet above the desert floor so sandstorms couldn't bury it. When another man, Hugh, took over driving, it was late at night. I went to sleep in back with all the others. The next thing I knew the truck was shaking and bouncing around violently, and I knew we'd gone off the road. Hugh had fallen asleep at the wheel. We were stuck in the desert with sand up to the axles of the truck.

The vehicle behind us had also stopped. The driver tried to help us out of the sand, but he only succeeded in burning out the clutch. Ours was a British-made truck and there was no way we could find parts in southern Iran. We ended up getting a big semi with a chain to pull us out of the sand and back onto the roadway. I was behind the wheel trying to steer, and it was such a sharp incline I thought for sure at one point the truck would turn over and I'd be killed. But we got back on track and the Persian driver towed us to a garage in the nearest town.

The mechanics there couldn't help us. I knew we had to take the clutch out and find another one, but that was going to be a problem. Dave Brown and I took the overnight bus up to Teheran — Dave had been in Iran once before and could speak a little Farsi. We carried the old part with us to the bazaar and went from shop to shop. Eventually we found what we needed and took the bus back the same night.

The whole incident delayed us about five days. Hugh felt guilty about falling asleep while he drove, and some people were beginning to act a little on edge with each other. I was still new enough as a Christian to feel some surprise that believers could be less than perfect!

When we did eventually get to Teheran, the alternator was starting to give us problems, so we stopped three or four more days while I repaired it. The group stayed in a church building. We had our devotional times as usual, but I knew my own relationship with the Lord wasn't what it should be. Nor were my companions all I thought they should be, spiritually! Somehow I had expected more from them.

From Teheran we drove straight to the Turkish border. We crossed in the mountains very late at night, and it was so cold that we stopped at a simple roadside cafe for hot soup. When we climbed back into the vehicles they wouldn't start! I didn't know what was wrong and began trying everything I could think of. Hours passed and dawn came. The other truck with us was working OK but mine still wasn't turning over. It was still very cold (we found out later it was minus 28 degrees Celsius) and we were getting desperate.

Finally we built a small fire under the fuel tank (safe enough with diesel). This eventually thinned the fuel enough to get it flowing and our truck came to life. I was still anxious about it and wanted to take off immediately. The others, however, decided they wanted some breakfast first and went back into the restaurant. When they came out and got back into the vehicle, the other truck suddenly quit! It had been idling very well until the moment. The driver, Al, guessed it might be the same problem with the fuel.

I thought our group should leave anyway but everyone else thought we should stay together. Al tried hard that whole day but he couldn't get his truck going until about 5:00 o'clock in the afternoon. Then we made it only a few miles up the mountain before both of our engines quit!

In those parts the winter sun goes down about 3:30 p.m. and temperatures plunge below freezing. There seemed to be no way to keep the fuel warm enough to keep us going. In addition to this problem, the electrical trouble I'd had before was starting to show up again. We were stuck on the mountainside all that night. The next day a few of us hiked into the next town and asked at a military base how we could get our vehicles towed in. This town had only about a thousand people, but it was the biggest one around. We didn't look very respectable after working on the vehicles but the people were extremely friendly and helpful. We were shown to the county office where they kept snowplows, and a man dispatched two machines to tow us off the side of the mountain.

The road was very narrow — and it was a long sheer drop off the edge. The two Turks who were towing us decided they'd have some fun by racing each other back to town. Our truck brakes weren't functioning very well. Visibility was poor since there was no heat to get the ice off the windows. But I will never forget looking out my left side window and catching sight of the ashen face of Al Bradley as his truck was towed past us. First one vehicle was in the lead and then the other one would overtake. I was expecting any moment to meet my Maker.

We survived this hair-raising adventure, however, and in town we found a place to stay and something to eat. The group bedded down for the night, ladies in one room, men in the other, while a few of us worked on the trucks. It was too late by then to get any fuel, but who should come by in a jeep just then but two American GI's from a nearby air force base. They spotted us as foreigners and stopped for a friendly conversation. When we explained that we needed to get a fire built under our two fuel tanks, they left and brought back some coal. We still had an electrical problem but I was so worn out and frustrated at that point that we decided to quit for that night.

Back at the hotel, I felt I had to do my Christian duty and have my devotions before I slept. Suddenly, however, as I picked up my Bible, my discouragement boiled over. I was disappointed with God. I felt betrayed. Christianity wasn't working the way I thought it should. I decided I wouldn't read the Bible any more, and threw it on the table. Then I went to bed, lying there depressed. After a while I began to realize the Lord was speaking to me. He was telling me that a relationship wasn't something that I did or that He did. I wasn't expected to be a puppet on a string and He wasn't a big Santa Claus in the sky. He wanted friendship, a personal relationship — exactly what I'd always hungered for! I went to sleep then, and the next morning when I saw my Bible lying there I picked it up and started reading. Somehow it was different. This book was talking about a real Person I was finally getting to know! It was the beginning of a whole new relationship.

We spent the next several days working on the vehicles and running into more frustrations. It took some time to get the parts we needed. I bought the biggest blowtorch I could find even though it cost a lot. Finally we got the trucks running properly.

As we set off again, we decided we would keep fires burning under the tanks all night. We used the coal the American soldiers had given us and whenever we stopped we men took stints watching the fires. We had decided to send the women in our group ahead of us by bus to Ankara, afraid they'd get too cold.

One night after I'd been sleeping for a couple of hours, some of the guys came shouting that the truck was on fire. All I wanted at that moment was to get on a train and go home. I heard myself say, *"Let it burn!"* But of course we got up and put the fire out. There really wasn't any damage. After that, the blowtorch thinned the fuel and kept us moving through the mountains.

Some days later I was with four guys in the back of the truck, just lying there thinking and talking with God. I'd been enjoying a greater closeness with Him recently than I'd ever felt in my life. I was finally beginning to understand that sometimes it's only through stress and brokenness that this happens. I remember saying to Him, *"I will go through all this again if I have to, and more, if I can learn more about You...!"* And the next thing I knew I was waking up in the snow, in excruciating pain.

From where I lay I could see the whole back of the truck had been ripped away. Everything we'd brought back from the ship was scattered over the hillside. A bus had stopped behind us, and people were rushing to help.

Harley Rollins had been driving the truck behind us and he'd seen everything. Our vehicle had simple hit a patch of ice and skidded, flipping over three times. The four of us in back hit the ceiling and the whole load had come down on top of us. Fortunately the roof fell off, or we would have been crushed.

My back had been injured and several ribs were broken where they joined the backbone. I remember people picking me up and putting me in the bus. I had to sit up and the pain was unbelievable. Three of us were taken to a hospital, a primitive place with few facilities and no attempt at hygiene; even the sheets had blood on them. We spent the next seven or eight days there and as foreigners we were a novelty. We hardly ever saw a doctor. I got some painkiller but even the needle looked dirty. John, an American guy with us, had been hit in the head. He was somewhat delirious and thought he was still in the galley of the ship! For days he just wandered around the hospital, eating nothing. To this day he doesn't remember any of it. Yet in spite of the fear and uncertainty about our situation, I felt a deep peace inside me. I had a sense that the Creator of the Universe was in control.

The hospital told us we'd have to stay for several weeks, but I wasn't about to do that. I rented a vehicle that would allow me to lie down in back, and the two of us who were left from our group got to the bus station. We took an overnight bus to Ankara and I stayed at the OM team leader's home for quite a number of weeks afterward, recuperating. By then, everybody else in the truck had gone on. Fortunately someone had found my passport in the debris of the accident and picked it up. I was grateful for that, even though I'd lost all my tools.

Each day that Dennis, the team leader, left his wife to go to work, I too had to leave for the sake of propriety. I teamed up with another man named Tom, who had also been left behind in Ankara to await the repair of his vehicle. When I began feeling better, we went together to the library at the British embassy or sightseeing to pass the time until my host returned home at night.

One of the problems I faced leaving the country was the fact that I no longer had the vehicle that I had registered in my passport as being in my possession. I wasn't supposed to leave Turkey without it. Of course my truck — or what was left of it — was still in eastern Turkey and unusable, but it had to be surrendered to customs. So another man, who was in the country working on translating the Bible into modern Turkish, went back with me. The customs officials told us we had to find someone we could give the vehicle to, so we found an orphanage and got the truck all properly written off.

When we got back to Ankara I found my friend Tom — who had been waiting for his vehicle to be repaired — still debating whether he should go on to India or return to Belgium. I didn't want to fly back to Belgium so we decided to drive the vehicle back together. It hadn't been repaired very well and the batteries were broken. In several cells, the acid had run out so it was difficult to start. The first morning after stopping for the night, we had trouble. After that we decided we would stop as little as possible, and at night park on a hill so we could start it more easily by putting it into gear.

Tom and I had covered a long part of the distance to Istanbul, when some loud banging sounds erupted. The hose pipe had gotten loose and jammed the radiator, and now it was leaking. It was very cold with snow on the ground. We weren't sure what to do, so we just prayed and asked God to help us with this problem. I talked to Him as though He was a close friend I could ask for help. As I finished praying, I saw a little discarded plastic bag by the side of the road. We poured some water into it from our canteens and filled up the radiator with this. Then we started driving again, stopping every few miles to check the leak. Everything seemed fine and we finally got all the way to Istanbul without leaking hardly any water at all! It seemed that the plastic bag had gotten hot and melted, blocking the holes in the radiator!

We wondered if we should stop in Istanbul and get the thing repaired properly. But it seemed to both of us that if God had brought us this far, we should take a step of faith and keep going, just allowing the Lord to work it out. And to make a long story short, we got all the way back to Belgium with the radiator as it was, only having to fill it up with water once in a while! That was another big lesson for me, another step in learning how I could trust the Lord.

On that trip I was not only dealing with physical struggles but also emotional ones. I learned that a girl I knew back at the base in Zaventem had suddenly died. The news had been kept from me in Ankara, but Tom told me and it was a shock. This girl was English, like I was, so we had been good friends. Of course, I didn't have the answers then and I still don't. It's all part of learning to trust.

When we reached the Turkish-Greek border, we received another blow. The officials who examined my passport refused to allow me through. They wanted to know where my vehicle was. We tried with English and a little German to explain what had happened with the truck, but they couldn't or wouldn't accept it. So we were stuck there all day while telephone calls were placed all around the country to different offices. It was another great frustration, but Tom and I kept praying. On retrospect I imagine the guards were probably expecting a bribe of some kind, but that never dawned on us. Eventually they let us through. On the Greek side we weren't allowed to exchange our Turkish lira for drachmas. This worried us because we thought we'd need diesel. We were finally directed to a bank that proved more willing.

By this time we were both feeling quite worn out. My back was still very painful — often after I took my turn driving I lay down in back. At the Yugoslav border, the guards became upset when we refused to switch off the engine. Of course we couldn't communicate enough to explain our concern. Then they started going through all the items we had in back. When they discovered a bag of flour they immediately decided we were drug smuggling! They tore the vehicle apart and we were there for hours. I don't even recall how the flour had gotten there — I think the ship's steward had sent it. We tried to give them the bag, tried to dump it out, but nothing did any good.

They were very excited. We thought for sure we'd be arrested and thrown into a Yugoslav jail! Only after many hours did they taste the flour and finally decide there were no drugs. We were free!

Passing through the Yugoslav border into Graz, Austria, the temperature grew very cold. It was December by this time, and I bitterly regretted the fact that all the heaters had been taken out of the vehicles going to India, in an effort to cut down on mechanical problems. Tom and I were excited over all God had done for us. At the same time we were physically and emotionally drained. But we made it through the roads of Austria, Germany and into Belgium, and drove at last into the yard of the base in Zaventem. *Home!* Our three-month odyssey was over.

Upon reflection I realized that God had made some major changes in me. My prayer life and Bible reading were different. So were my plans for the future. There was a fundamental change in my perception of God and the Christian life. I had walked through some valleys and come out at the other end with much more joy and contentment. And I knew that if I could see God at work in the same way, I would turn around and go through it all over again. That was the beginning of my OM life.

About a year after that first trip, I was asked to drive overland again. I picked and prepared the truck myself, hoping this time to prevent some of the difficulties of the past. But after many years and many trips later, I can honestly say that no matter what measures you take, God will allow hundreds of other accidents, breakdowns, arrests, and incidents to come your way —you just need to learn to trust Him! Taking us out of control is sometimes the only way for him to teach us that He is in control.

This is the way of faith.

17

When All Else Fails

by Captain Graeme Bird

*E*stimated time of arrival (ETA) of the *MV Doulos* in our next Southeast Asian port-of-call was 09.00 on 9 May 1996.

The pilot boarded at 08.30. Upon making his appearance on the bridge his first order was, "Hard Starboard!" to cut some distance off my intended course. My track was laid down to pass to the east of a shoal (shallow water). It is quite normal for pilots to change courses like that, but it does raise questions. My first one was obvious.

"Do you know there is a shoal?" I asked politely. The answer was comfortingly calm. "Yes, I do know. It's quite OK."

The cadet, meanwhile, had hoisted the pilot flag. The pilot approached me and requested that the flag be taken down, because he is not the pilot. This man had just come to my bridge and ordered hard-a-starboard heading near a shoal, and now he informs me that he is not a pilot! I managed to restrain myself from asking whether he is the butcher, baker or candlestick maker. The man explained that he was a private pilot, but doing this job for free. My composure and smile returned.

Standing on the bridge wing, steering up on the berth, I asked about the tugs that I ordered.

"They haven't turned up yet," came the reply. "Ships don't normally use tugs anyway, because the tug drivers don't know what to do."

My composure faded but quickly returned as I decided we could berth using an anchor. The forward mooring station was notified and the starboard anchor prepared. Our berth was looming closer.

"What is our hull strength like?" the pilot suddenly demanded.

My thoughts took off, but I confined myself to a single succinct question. "Why?"

"The berth is shallow at the forward part. At low tide your bow may touch bottom," he revealed.

Bearing in mind that we were in our final approach I decided to keep my response as brief and non-technical as possible. "That is NOT good!"

The pilot seemed rather surprised by this hostile reaction. "Oh," he said. "My decision to not go too far into the berth but rather stay near the seaward end seemed prudent."

Tugs are a great invention, and to my relief one turned up to assist. Ordinarily the immediate response of the bridge – especially as the berth is coming into clear view and is in fact very close – is to inform the tug of its duties and give specific instructions. This is usually done through VHF radio. But as the pilot and I watched with utter disbelief the tug skipper signaled to indicate that he had no radio.

Prayer is a mighty tool and by now I was making good use of it. The ship was almost at the berth, the tug had no radio, the berth had no water, and the pilot wasn't really a pilot. What else could go wrong?

One should never ask such a question without bracing for a reply. By now the tug had left us and gone to the linesmen on the wharf to pick up a hand-held VHF radio. The skipper then commenced to push our ship as instructed by the pilot. He started to push too much and our bow started heading too quickly towards the berth. I negotiated with the pilot, letting him know that it would be very good to let go our anchor now. He really didn't want to but I insisted. Our bow slowed down its swing, but we did need to stop going forward or else we would crash into a roll-on-roll-off ramp worth many thousands of dollars.

"Slow astern," the cadet repeated the order to the engine room, but nothing happened. The pilot then ordered "Full astern!" Again the engine failed to respond.

I am not used to running around the bridge, mainly because there is no space to run. But on this occasion I managed to get to the engine telegraph very quickly and slam it into "double full astern." Afterwards I realized how hard I had slammed it because the indicator lever was dislodged. God has given us creative minds. By now all I could imagine was a destroyed ramp and one very badly damaged bow. The only consoling thought was that the ramp had been raised high enough that impact would not cause damage below the water-line. This removed the danger of flooding our lower sections.

My prayer life had increased tenfold by this point in time and I realized the pilot was totally oblivious to what was happening. Suddenly the phone rang. "That'll be Bryce," I thought knowingly. As Chief Engineer he would be ringing to say all was fixed, we had full power, we were saved. Instead of his voice, however, I heard the sweet and innocent voice of the ship's receptionist. "Has the pilot left?" she wanted to know. "Is it all right to page now?"

Responses unworthy of a Christian ran through my poor racked brain. Why in the world didn't the girl look outside and see if we were tied up? I managed a strangled "NO!" and slammed the phone into its cradle.

Somehow, miraculously, the third mate managed to hold on to our anchor. Disaster was narrowly averted. There was no grinding crunch, only some scraped paint on the hull. The ship's company was excited to arrive in yet another port. The "pilot" remained unaware of exactly what had been going on. The captain...well, his heartbeat was still settling down. His color was slowly returning to normal. And as he prepared himself for the adventures that undoubtedly lay ahead, he was deeply thankful that God is Master of all – and quite capable of answering multiple prayers, all at the same time!

HIS
HEALING
TOUCH

18

Open My Eyes, Lord!

by Stella Chan

I was serving aboard the *MV Logos* when we sailed the South China Sea and rescued more than 80 Vietnamese "boat people." Some of the refugees suffered from fever, eye disease or skin disease. This added a big burden to our ship's medical team, which was run by a doctor and a nurse. I was working with the ministry department, planning programs, but by profession I am a registered nurse and midwife. I was glad to use my free time to help on the medical side. However, I never dreamed that I would become a patient myself!

I was sharing a cabin with Joy, an American woman. One night I was awakened from sleep by sharp pains in both my eyes. I could not open them, so I used my fingers to pry up my right eyelid. The pain increased in intensity and tears poured down my face. I was shocked, realizing that something was seriously wrong. Quietly I cried out to the Lord, asking for his help.

It was the middle of the night. Everyone was sound asleep and I had no idea what I should do. I determined not to waste my pain. I knew my Master must have a lesson in this and asked him to teach me whatever he wanted me to learn. In my heart

91

I started to sing songs to praise and thank Him for His love and His suffering for me on the cross. I told him He was the Lord of my life, and thanked Him for the 32 years I had been able to use my eyes. I said that I was willing to accept whatever He decided was best for me, knowing His grace was sufficient.

When Joy woke up and saw me she was alarmed — each eye had swollen to the size of an egg!

The ship at that time was tied up in Bangkok, Thailand. Dr. Chong, the ship's doctor, tried to go ashore and find an eye specialist but he was unsuccessful. "Stella, I honestly do not know what's wrong with your eyes. The eye pressure is normal. Let us pray, and I will put in some eye drops and try some medicine."

He applied the medication and we prayed. I know the whole crew prayed as I lay in my bed during the next days, feeling physically exhausted. I could not open my eyes and lived in the dark. Still, my heart rested upon my God.

On the second evening our captain came to visit me in my cabin. He told me that Dr. Chong's medical report said that my eyes were in critical condition. With a firm but gentle voice he asked, "Stella, do you believe in prayer for healing, and shall I pray for you?"

I assured the captain that I would welcome his prayer. He knelt down on the floor beside me and put his hands upon my eyes. Then he spoke a few simple words, asking the Lord to touch me.

And that's exactly what God did. For the first time the next morning I was able to open my eyes. They were still very red, however, so I whispered another prayer.

"Lord, I know you've touched me. Can you please let my eyes return to the proper color in three hours' time? If they do I can attend a meeting which is important for the ministry on board."

Every half-hour I looked anxiously into the mirror to see if there was a change. Just before the meeting was due to start, my eyes cleared!

I left the _Logos_ in 1981. In my autograph book Dr. Chong remarked upon our "very interesting experiences" together. Then he added: "Remember your swollen eyes? I am surely glad that our Lord is the sovereign God, — and that you got well, in spite of my treatment!"

So am I, dear Dr. Chong. Neither of us ever doubted what made the difference, back during those days when human help was not enough. It was the touch of the Master.

19

King of Hearts

by Alfy Franks

During the Seventies we had a man with a great burden to work for God in North India. At one point this man, Nelson George, fell ill and became increasingly weak. Doctors examined him and sent him to a cardiologist. This specialist afterward called Ron Penny, who was then the leader of the work in Bihar where Nelson was. He told him that Nelson was very seriously ill and probably had only about ten days to live. His heart was so enlarged there was nothing medical science could do for him.

Ron did not tell Nelson, only suggested that he go home and take a month's rest and see the doctors there. Nelson went home, traveling almost three days by train. When he went to see a cardiologist, the latter told him to return after another three days, when he had had sufficient time to rest from his long trip. Then, he said, he would start Nelson on some medication.

Nelson was so weak at this point that his church was alarmed. Members began to fast and pray. When we in Bombay heard the news that Nelson had an enlarged heart and Ron Penny revealed the seriousness of his condition, we also fasted

95

and prayed continuously. After three days, Nelson went back to see the specialist.

The man was stunned by his patient's obvious improvement. Later, he admitted that when he had first seen Nelson he doubted that he would live beyond another ten or so hours.

"That is why I told you to come back after three days! — I felt there was no point in examining you when it was so apparent that you were not going to live for very long. Why go through all the hassle of medications that were not going to do any good?"

The doctor kept looking at Nelson as though he were a ghost. Then he examined him. The evidence was indisputable.

"God has definitely healed you," stated the cardiologist simply.

To Nelson the news was no great surprise. Medical science had its limitations, but God knew all about human hearts. There wasn't one the Lord couldn't heal in answer to His children's prayers.

20

God Is Enough

by Greg Kernaghan

*W*hen we were criss-crossing cultures by sea and land on the *MV Doulos* and *MV Logos,* my wife Anni and I were privileged to see God's hand at work in many ways. Our lifestyle created a high degree of corporate dependence on God's merciful intervention and it was natural to speak of our hope being "God or nothing". Yet it was a different test entirely when we faced our greatest personal crisis.

Having lost our first child through a miscarriage, our excitement, nervousness and hope grew perhaps faster than the new child we awaited in the spring of 1983. Anni's first six months of pregnancy passed without event. Then, on a rough voyage from the Faroe Islands to Bergen, Norway, serious problems suddenly arose. Anni had to be hospitalized. The following day *Logos* sailed on to its next port-of-call. I stood on the quayside, feeling absolutely alone

But God had foreseen everything and His plans were already in motion. I was introduced to a local Christian family who was willing to host us for as long as necessary. This was not just any family, for I learned that six years before the couple had gone through the identical experience that we were now entering. Their daughter was born in the same nearby hospital, one of the finest university research facilities for premature babies in Scandinavia. The six-year-old's lively presence gave me hope.

The diagnosis, however, was not encouraging. Both Anni and the child within were in grave danger. The doctors' priority was to prevent the toxic effects of pre-eclampsia and other complications from causing permanent liver damage to Anni. Her blood pressure rose to dangerous levels.

Tests showed that the child, approaching 28 weeks, had not grown in two weeks. The umbilical cord was wrapped twice around his neck. The pregnancy had to be terminated.

On May 19, our son, Jaakko, was removed from his mother's womb and whisked away to the Premature Intensive Care Unit where he would spend the next 11 weeks. He was given a 10% chance of survival with no regard to normal development. He weighed only 900 grams and was 37 centimeters in length; my hand formed an ample cradle.

I rushed to Anni's side but she was not yet in the mood for guests. So I returned to see "my son" — that phrase tasted good! There he lay in an incubator, so covered with wires and tape and monitors that he was nearly hidden. I instantly realized why he could have used another three months in the womb. Besides being tiny he had no fat whatsoever; his skin tore like paper when sensors were changed. He spent eleven days on a respirator which bloated his abdomen like a frog. Milk was pumped into his stomach round the clock. Every biological function was scrutinized. None of this made him seem real. I hovered near him, afraid even to touch him.

I will be forever grateful to the wise doctor who saw my reaction. "Wash your hands and pick him up", he instructed. "He's your son and you both need each other."

I cannot describe the transformation that followed. The tiny fist that instinctively grabbed my finger became, to me, an invitation to place this child in God's keeping. Whatever the future held, we were one and that could not be taken away!

Anni had not been able to experience this vital bonding, for she had not yet seen Jaakko. She was not recovering as the doctors had hoped. Ten days after his birth I was thrilled to be able to take her to "meet" him, hold him, and weep in joy over him. Her own recovery accelerated from that moment.

Jaakko's eleven weeks in Intensive Care was unquestionably the most intense period of my life. Our visits were the focus of each day. Whenever Anni and I weren't with him, the ringing of the telephone made us sick with apprehension.

But strangely, neither Anni nor I tried to demand healing or life, either for her or our son. At that "flash point" of faith when we felt that everything we leaned on was being stripped away, we still knew that we loved God deeply and wanted to please Him, come what may. God Himself was all we really would ever need.

We also discovered that, in the heat of crisis, one quickly runs out of ways to pray and is reduced simply to watching and waiting. Our own hearts were so overwhelmed we could not carry the burden any longer. But we knew with a certainty that a prayer network spanned the globe, interceding for us. To this day, I still meet people who have never met Jaakko and yet feel they know him because of their prayers.

There were several tense moments during those weeks and, in fact, for the first two years in Jaakko's life. Yet there remained a strong conviction on the part of many friends that God had a purpose for Jaakko's life. I have never forgotten that.

Two years later, our daughter was born under similar, yet less threatening, circumstances. Maria weighed 1800 grams, which seemed tiny to most people but twice as large to us! Good things DO come in small packages! Today Jaakko and Maria are "normal" teenagers and we are likely "normal" parents of teenagers. But we are still awed whenever we remember God's goodness and touch upon our lives.

21

It's Not an Easy Road!

by May Huay Ho

*F*or nine years I had wanted to travel overland and work in Bangladesh. The year I decided to go ahead, the doors were not only open, they were falling off their hinges! Everything was almost too easy. On my way to Brussels to get my visas, I prayed and said to the Lord, *"I can't believe this. People who want to go to the Muslim world have all kinds of battles. Why is it so easy for me?"*

As soon as I said *"Amen"* the car I was traveling in crashed into the car in front of us. The accident took place just as we were passing our car insurance company office. We were sent immediately to the nearest hospital — one of the top eye hospitals in the world

I was the only one seriously injured in the crash and I needed an eye operation. The night after my operation, I was in tremendous pain. I remember lying there, wondering if I was going to lose my sight. Then I had a dream and I heard these words clearly: "I know that my Redeemer lives... I myself will see Him, with my own eyes. — I and not another!" Afterwards I found those words written in the Bible, Job 19:27, and knew God was giving me His personal reassurance that I wouldn't be blind.

For the next two months I had double vision. I finally got to Bangladesh the following January, although I still have some numbness on half my face even today. Sometimes I think of Jacob, in the Bible. Every time he limped around he must have been reminded of the moment he wrestled with God. Every time I touch my face, I remember my accident.

Years later I told my story to a Christian surgeon who said that I was a very lucky girl. Most European doctors, he explained, don't have extensive experience with the size and shape of Asian eyes. And when the eye is swollen it is very difficult for a surgeon to be 100% accurate.

No luck involved at all! —God knew what He was doing. I have no problems with my vision as my journey continues, one step at a time, one day at a time, one year at a time. When I fall, I know my Lord is there, ready to help me pick myself back up.

22

Precious Seed

by Debbie Meroff

When little Danielle Shugart died with lightning suddenness from acute leukemia in June of 1990, a huge chunk of the Shugart family's world came crashing down. During their four years in Pakistan, they had fielded a great many of the Enemy's "flaming arrows." A couple of years before, they survived the explosion of an ammunition dump near their house. This, the death of a beloved child, was hardest of all.

Ten months later, they celebrated the birth of another daughter, Sophia. Craig and Krista Shugart's joy, however, was immediately shadowed by anxiety.

"I don't think it ever crossed our minds, or at least settled in our hearts, that we were disadvantaged or ripped off. There was some fear as implications for the future set in, but in the midst of it God gave us satisfaction in what He had done. Sophia's birth improved the quality of our lives. We don't minimize the difficulties, but we don't let ourselves get bogged down in them."

After Sophia's birth, Craig continued teaching math and chemistry in a private school in Pakistan. The next year he was offered the prestigious post of headmaster of a major boy's high school.

But Satan was ready with yet another unexpected assault. Craig developed a lesion in one ear that was diagnosed as a malignant melanoma: skin cancer.

"This type of melanoma is rare — and almost always fatal unless they catch it in time. The doctors felt they had. The only treatment is to cut off the affected skin tissue. They told me that if another lesion ever appeared it meant the cancer had invaded internally and there was no hope."

Some months later, another lesion did appear. Although it seemed futile, Craig was immediately scheduled for surgery. Friends around the world prayed. And something totally inexplicable — by medical standards — occurred. When he reported to doctors in Canada for the appointed surgery, they discovered that the lesion had disappeared. There was no more trace of the melanoma.

The Shugart family was happy to return to Pakistan. Life was not easy. Krista had to work hard with Sophia, helping her with special programs. But according to Craig, God gifted her with a great love for children and an appreciation of what "quality of life" really means.

"We still miss Dani," he admitted. "Hardly a day goes by that the family doesn't recall her, that she's alive with God." But the Lord actually gave Krista a premonition before she died. He spoke through the verse, 'Unless a kernel of wheat falls to the ground and dies, it remains only a single seed. But if it dies, it produces many seeds.' The Lord told Krista clearly that Dani was that seed. She was our 'down payment' for the work in Pakistan. We can't walk away from that."

HIS
PRACTICAL
TOUCH

23

SOS

by Penny Davison
(Name changed for security reasons.)

*W*e were leading a team in Northern Iraq that was rebuilding homes for Kurds who had lost everything during the Gulf War. When a dispute arose in one of the villages we were working in, the engineer responsible for that village agreed to travel out with me to try to sort it out.

Before leaving for the village, we stopped at the supply warehouse to tank up. Our vehicle was running low on gasoline, not enough for a return trip to the village, which was a few hours' distance. Gas stations were non-existent in this war-torn part of the world, so fuel had to be brought in from across the borders and stored. Unfortunately, it turned out that our agency had not received its quota of fuel and the tanks in the warehouse were empty, too. The warehouse supervisor, aware of our need, assured us that they would send a taxi out to collect us later.

The engineer and I successfully completed the meeting in the village, then started back for town. Just as we had anticipated, the van came to a sputtering halt, with the fuel indicator on zero. It was the middle of the day, the hottest time.

There was no one around; we had no water and no idea when the promised taxi would arrive. So I sent a simple and silent call to God for help.

Almost immediately my Kurdish companion, Ali, turned and demanded to know if I had prayed. When I nodded his eyes grew wide and he grabbed my hand. *"I believe!"* he cried, *"I believe!"*

Not sure what he was going on about, I asked him what it was that he believed. He pointed to the fuel tank indicator. Then he said, *"Anything you say about your God, I believe!"*

I looked across at the fuel gauge and finally understood. The indicator needle had moved. It was now pointing to one-third full! I turned the key in the ignition and the van took us all the way back to town without a problem.

Ali and I were not the only astonished ones. The men at the warehouse had checked the fuel gauge before we left, and were concerned because they had not been able to send a taxi after us. Ali shared the story with them too.

The engineer and his wife did begin to study the Bible with us after that. And soon they really did believe in Jesus Christ. When Saddam Hussein re-took Northern Iraq in the summer of 1996, they were among the many endangered Kurds who left the country to make a new start in the West.

24

Guiding Our Footsteps

Contributed by Rosemary Hack

Bible Correspondence Courses are a vital way to share the gospel in many countries. In the Sudan, lessons by mail allow Muslims to investigate Christianity without attracting unwanted attention. The ministry began three years ago and the number of students is steadily growing.

Isaac, coordinator of the correspondence course work, is also an evangelist. Whenever possible, he visits students to discuss their progress and answer questions. Of course, since the Sudan is a Muslim country, he has to be discreet.

One time Isaac set out to visit a student in an unfamiliar city. Although he had a name and address, there was no street map to follow, and streets were not neatly labeled. Isaac didn't want to ask a lot of questions. Finally, he just stopped his wandering and prayed that God would lead him in the right direction. Then he approached a nearby person.

"Oh!" exclaimed the man, in answer to his question. "The house you are looking for is here!"

Isaac was astounded. He was standing right in front of the place he had been seeking.

25

Prayer Fuel

by Rex Worth

*B*ack when I was Chief Engineer on the *Logos,* we were always looking for cheap fuel. One time George Verwer, the ship's director, heard of some that was available in Jeddah. Christian ships don't usually go to Saudi Arabia, but we went along there and dropped the anchor.

The next day a barge came out with fuel. For the first time I could remember in my career at sea, this barge had brought the wrong fuel! We couldn't use it. The captain on board leaped up and down and told me I should take what he had, but of course I refused. The barge went away, we waited another day, and finally the right barge came out with a German captain. This man started talking with Manfred Schaller, also from Germany, who really witnessed to this guy. He became very interested and gave us quite a bit of extra fuel. It was so cheap, I thought it was a fantastic opportunity. George wasn't anywhere on board to consult so we pumped out the ballast from number three tank and filled everything right up to the gunwales with this cheap fuel. I was quite pleased with myself. The barge went away and a launch appeared with the agent. I told him the figures of how much fuel we had taken and away he went.

Still no George! We were all wondering where he was when finally, after a long wait, we saw a high-speed launch suddenly come out from shore. I could see Verwer sitting there with steam coming out of his ears! As soon as he got on deck he began chewing me out.

"Who told you to take so much fuel?"

"Well," I said defensively, "it was cheap!"

"Yes, I know it's cheap, but this was a cash deal — *Only* cash. That's why it was so cheap!"

He began calming down a little, explaining, "I had all the cash ready in a brown paper carrier bag, and then I left it on the ship! What could I do? I turned to the Muslim man who was selling us the cheap fuel and said, 'Excuse me, sir, I know it's Thursday. Could you possibly take a check, and wait until Monday to cash it?'

"The man said, 'Yes, no problem, I'll wait until Monday.'"

So now George said to me, "Call everybody on this ship to prayer! We do not have enough money to cover that check. I signed it in faith!"

So we all put in some serious prayer time. By Monday morning that money had come in from different places. Every penny of the bill was paid.

❖   ❖   ❖

Another time on the *MV Doulos,* in Vera Cruz, we couldn't get any fuel and neither could any other ship. They were all sailing up the coast to get it. George Miley was the director then. He called me to his cabin and asked, "Rex, how far can we go? We've got to get fuel." So I went back down to the cabin to work things out and calculated just how far we could go.

Then I got hold of my wife Ros and said, "This is God's ship. Let's pray. Because if God wants us to go anywhere, He's got to put something in the tank." We got on our knees in our cabin and prayed hard. I said, "Either you do something, Lord, or we stop here." We got off our knees and I told Ros I'd take the figures up to George Miley and tell him how far we could go. I came out of the cabin, looked over the side, and there was this little pickup truck with hoses, connecting up our hoses. We were the only ship in that port that had ordered fuel that actually got it!

Engineers always take a sample of what's coming aboard. I had four sample bottles on my desk and all four were different colors. I'd never seen anything like it before in my life! Nobody knew where the fuel came from or what color it was supposed to be. But God had provided exactly what we needed.

26

Making Crooked Places Straight

by Rex Worth

We had a generator on the Doulos that nearly broke my heart. The thing should have been thrown overboard years before. When it finally broke down one day, we took out the camshaft and put it in the lathe. We could see it was bent like a donkey's hind leg.

The guys came to me and asked, "What do we do, Rex?" I said, "I honestly don't know, but I know a Man who does." And we got around that lathe in our boiler suits, covered in oil and grease, and we had the best prayer meeting I've ever known. We said, "Lord, this is your ship. Show us what we're supposed to do with this thing. It's so bent we can't use it and we don't know what to do."

We put up chain blocks from the deck head, welded pads on the deck with ratchet blocks, and bent this thing the opposite way! Of course this idea was totally impossible. Any engineer will tell you that. Then we said, "Right, stop. Let's pray." We got around that thing and we prayed again. Then we took off the tension, the chain blocks and ratchet blocks. I told a Swiss boy to put a level on it. It was perfectly straight, the full length of that shaft. We put in new bearings and it ran for years more after that. Impossible — but not for the God of Creation!

115

27

Short Circuit

by Stan Thompson

I had served as Chief Electrical Officer in the British Navy, then on cruise liners and some time on freighters. In 1974 George Verwer recruited me as a chief electrician for the *Logos*. After a year, my job changed to lining-up ship visits, but when the possibility of a second ship came along, OM leaders asked if I would serve as the Chief Electrician during the time of refitting and commissioning.

The ship under consideration was the *Franca C,* a Costa Line Cruise ship that was being retired. As a Chief Electrician, I had the privilege of going with the team of Chief Engineer, Captain, Chief Steward and Marine Superintendent to sail aboard the *Franca C* for her last cruise. We checked out the technical side of things as the ship sailed from Venice around the Greek islands to Genoa. When the rest of the OM team left after that to make a bid for the *Franca C,* I stayed on board on my own. Of course I was busily picking the brains of the electricians and finding out all I could about the technicalities of the ship, in case we did buy it, so I could be a jump ahead on the electrics. Of course we eventually got this ship, which became the *Doulos,* and took it round from Genoa to Bremen, Germany.

In Bremen I oversaw the electrical part of the refitting. We finally got to the stage where we had gotten everything overhauled and all was ready to receive our safety certificates. The safety surveyor was coming the following morning. At five o'clock that afternoon, however, a fault suddenly developed. Of all things, it was the emergency lighting system, a very basic and essential requirement for getting a safety certificate!

There were five electricians serving under me. I'd been on ships for many years, knew the idiosyncrasies with these old direct-current system ships. We searched and searched and couldn't find why the circuit breaker was tripping out. The fault could have been anywhere — there were dozens of emergency light fittings all over the ship. Even if we worked all night we could never take them all down before the next morning, when this man was due to arrive. We didn't even know where to begin. There were no circuit diagrams and whatever there was, was in Italian. We worked until about 6:00 p.m. Then I told the guys to go to supper and we would resume work afterwards.

After they had gone I went into one of the former passenger cabins and prayed. I said, *"Lord, Your Word tells me that You are the Creator of all things, things seen and things unseen. Lord, I realize that also includes the structure of matter, of atoms and the atmosphere and everything else.*

"Lord you know our problem. It's so basic, but we're not able to solve it. You know the urgency of the situation. Will You please help us, Lord, to find this fault?"

I came out of that cabin and walked up the port side of the main deck toward the stairs that go up to the dining room. I crossed the front of the stairs to the starboard part of the ship, walked right along the passageway, and went down the steps to the deck below. I cannot tell you why. I just had an inward compulsion to do this. I went to the end of the alleyway down there, and there was a long, fluorescent fitting on the deck head.

The emergency lighting was incandescent, inside the fluorescent fitting. One was DC current and the other AC. I went into a cabin and got a bunk ladder so I could climb up and take down the four-foot fluorescent fitting. Then I stripped the whole thing off. And where the wires came through the hole in the bulkhead, I could see a black mark. I sniffed — and caught the definite smell of burned electrical insulation. I pulled out those wires. There they were, burned through. There was our short circuit.

Our God is a practical God. He answered my "telegraph prayer" and proved He is Lord — even of burnt-out wires, and electricians!

28

A President Paves the Way

by Stephen Hart

*T*he riverboat wasn't much to look at. According to locals, the vessel had sunk twice and burned once. But the OM team decided that if it could stay afloat for the two weeks they needed it in late December, it would do. Their dream of mounting an exhibition of Christian books in Khartoum, the capital of Sudan, was about to come true.

Besides renting the boat, the team reserved and paid for a mooring on the busy side of the Nile River, right next to a main roadway in the town center. What a place to reach the crowds! But when they steamed up, the local officials refused to let them come in. "Too shallow," was their excuse. Disconsolate, the OMers were forced to withdraw to the opposite side of the river where far fewer people passed by. *"How will we ever draw people here,"* they wondered. They prayed and asked the Lord for help.

And God answered — *with a landslide!* A quarter of a mile up the river, a stretch of the bank slid down into the Nile, washing out the footpath. The President of Sudan himself went to inspect the damage, accompanied by a military escort and TV cameras. While he was there he noticed a boat moored a little further down the shore. Strings of lights decorated the

121

vessel and loud speakers blared music and messages. "What's this?" the president wondered. He and his party sauntered over for a look, with TV cameras following.

When OM's "motley crew" saw the military delegation approach they were sure it was the end of everything. But an officer introduced them to the president, and they were pleased to give him a "royal" tour, crowning it with the presentation of a Bible. The president appeared greatly pleased and kissed the Bible — a common gesture of respect for a holy book, and conveying his response that he accepted the gift with pleasure.

The TV cameras recorded everything, and that evening all the viewers in Khartoum watched it on their screens. The next morning a photograph of the Bible presentation was splashed on the front pages of leading newspapers. For days afterwards, the boat was swamped with visitors! The team not only saw a huge sale of Christian Literature in Arabic and English, but they had scores of friendly conversations with the local populace. Before the two-week event was over, at least five visitors professed faith in Jesus Christ. Thanks to a mudslide, they didn't miss the boat!

29

The Case of The Missing Passport

by Torleif Sorlie

It had been a long and tiring drive from Madrid to Seville, in the southern part of Spain. Finally Ronnie and I pulled up in front of a hostel called "Buen Dormir," Good Sleep, in the old part of Seville. As we parked the car outside the rundown building we were immediately informed by a bystander that we had been observed. Thieves were eagerly waiting for us to leave our foreign and attractive vehicle unattended.

The dire warning did not stop us from going inside to claim a room. Just as we were ready to stretch our tired backs upon beds covered with holed sheets, the owner of the hostel knocked. He had been kind enough to fill in the registration papers. All we needed to do was sign at the bottom of the page. I briefly looked over my form. To my surprise, somebody else's name was on it! Was the man trying to trick me? It was easy to suspect anyone in this part of town. I quickly glanced at the red Norwegian passport. It was red and it was Norwegian, sure enough. – But it wasn't mine. I had never seen the person whose photograph was inside! What was going on?

Ronnie and I were on a survey trip to Operation Mobilization's ship, the *MV Doulos,* It was our job to visit all the port

123

cities along the coast of Spain, making appointments with port authorities, city officials and church leaders, The purpose was to find out which ports would welcome a visit by a unique ship like the *Doulos*. Our survey was scheduled to take five weeks, allowing just a few nights in each town.

Our first main stop had been in Barcelona. After some time with our OM team there we went on to Madrid for discussions with the shipping agent representative. This person would be handling some of the practical details of the ship's visit in each port. Since my colleague, Ronnie, couldn't drive and I couldn't speak Spanish, we were a perfect pair for this assignment.

In Madrid we enjoyed a delicious meal in a Swiss restaurant, compliments of our agent, then headed for our inexpensive hostel in the city center. Regulations required that we hand in our passports when we checked in, and receive them back in the morning. It was at that point that the case of the missing passport got underway. When Ronnie got his black passport and I my red one in Madrid, neither of us thought to check them. It was only many kilometers and hours later that we realized there had been two Norwegians staying in that hostel. - And the receptionist had gotten us confused!

What should we do? We needed to go almost immediately to Portugal, so we would need our passports. Trying to see the comical side of it we had a good laugh. Then we discussed the best solution. The other Norwegian concerned might have already left the hostel without checking his passport, and who could know where he was headed? We decided to go to the police for help. It was already 10 p.m. when we started our search for the nearest police station. After finding one we were obliged to wait in a big, cold room with bruised and handcuffed criminals who had been brought in that evening. But our wait was in vain. The police were unable or unwilling to help. We did have the telephone number of the hostel in Madrid, but by this time it was too late to call.

The following morning I phoned Madrid. The other Norwegian was still staying at the hostel, I learned to my relief. The man had gone out with his passport, probably to change money, so we waited and phoned again. Eventually I was able to speak to my compatriot. We agreed that he would send my passport to our agent in Cadiz, which was a bit further down the list of Spanish ports to visit. I would post his passport back to the hostel.

That part of the problem was solved. – But what about going to Portugal? It would still take days for my passport to arrive and we had appointments to keep. We decided to go on to a city on the Spanish border. I would stay in a hostel there while Ronnie took a ferry over to the Portuguese side, and spoke to officials.

At every hostel we came to we were asked to present our passports. Nobody was willing to take in a suspicious foreigner like me without one! So we opted for Plan B. We phoned a pastor in the area and explained our situation, then asked if he could provide accommodation for us for the night. The pastor said he would check with members of his congregation. We were to call back in half an hour. Since Spain does not have a lot of evangelical churches, our contacts were limited. Unfortunately, nobody at this particular church could offer hospitality at such short notice. We were stranded once again.

In our state of desperation we turned to the Lord. After a time of prayer in the car, outside the telephone booth, we again discussed the situation, I volunteered to spend a couple of days and nights in the car while Ronnie went over to Portugal, but he did not feel good about that. We decided to try again to look for accomodation. Walking through the dirty, littered streets of the unappealing town of Huelva, we asked for a room at the cheapest-looking hostel. Even they refused us! Finally we found a place that only asked for one passport. We phoned our ship headquarters to explain why Mission Portugal was not yet complete, and got another surprise. Further research had turned up the fact that the harbor of the Portuguese port we were going to visit was too small for our ship to enter. Our survey trip there would have been a waste of time!

Hopefully our missing passport would be awaiting us at our next stop. We carried on to Cadiz with anticipation. At the beach we stopped to take a stroll along the wet sand and enjoy the refreshing sea breeze. This might have been the happy ending to our tale, were it not for the sight that greeted us when we returned to our car. To our horror the side window was smashed – and Ronnie's jacket with his passport was missing! Now there were two of us without passports!

A moment later a police car parked nearby approached us. The officers explained they had become suspicious earlier, seeing a man running down the street, and caught him with a jacket containing the passport. He was now sitting handcuffed in their car.

Off we went to the police station to file a report. Not that it would help us much. Our window was smashed, and the only thing we could do was go to a Ford dealer and buy a new one. At the garage we were told that our model of car was unusual in Spain and they might not be able to find an exact replacement window. After some phoning around they reported they had located one, but it was tinted. Since a dark window is better than no window at all, we agreed.

The next morning we went to pick up the car. The replacement window was a perfect match to the others! The manager announced that just as they were about to put in the tinted window, a man had driven up to the garage with the exact same Ford model as ours. When he learned what was happening he had offered to exchange his own clear window for the tinted version!

Our trip through Spain was not yet over. The Lord had more lessons about His faithful provision on the road ahead. Yet as we continued along the coast that day with both of the missing passports safely in our pockets and a new window for the car, we had no doubt about who was in control.

HIS
PROVIDING
TOUCH

30

Lessons of the Road

by Chacko Thomas
as told to Anne Buchanan Kammies

*I*t was the middle of India's monsoon season. Each day, torrential rainfall made it extremely difficult for the OM team to carry on their usual program of open-air evangelism and door-to-door work. Adding to the problem of poor weather was the fact that they were working in an extremely resistant area. Book sales were poor — and the men depended on sales to pay their living expenses.

The team's temperamental means of transportation was a seven-ton truck with an air leak in the system. Every four or five miles the engine would suddenly cut out. The men would then be forced to get down in the pouring rain, pump the air out of the engine, and then push-start it — because the starter wasn't working properly either. At this time of year, most of the roads had turned into a quagmire of mud and clay — not the easiest surface for push-starting a heavy truck loaded with literature, especially when the procedure had to be repeated every few miles!

At this point the team had completely run out of funds. The time had come to move on to the next town for ministry,

129

but they had no money to buy fuel for the thirty-mile journey. Undeterred, they drove to the main road and waited. Team leader Chacko Thomas collected a small stack of evangelistic books, and when the next truck approached, he stepped out into the road to stop it. Chacko held up the pile of books and explained the situation to the driver, asking if he could trade the books for some fuel. The Hindu driver agreed and proceeded to syphon some of the fuel from his tank into the OM truck.

With this transaction complete, and a certain sense of accomplishment, the team once more push-started their vehicle and drove off into the rain. Their driver was an Englishman named John Miles. At this stage, John's main concern was to keep the truck moving at a steady pace in order to avoid further breakdowns.

They were well on their way to their destination when just ahead they saw a young buffalo calf step onto the road. The animal began to amble across at a leisurely pace, but John was reluctant to decelerate, as the truck would most certainly stall. He quickly decided his best option was to swing to the right and pass around the buffalo. This strategy might have been successful had the animal not chosen that moment to stop dead in its tracks. Truck and buffalo collided with a sickening thud. The latter was thrown off the road into a rice field, were it lay motionless.

The team got out to assess the situation. In no time at all, the entire population of the nearby village had descended, the men carrying long sticks and the women wailing and screaming. The death or injury of an animal like this was a calamity, both economically and religiously. Hindus believed that cows carried the reincarnated souls of loved ones. Everyone stood around staring at the little buffalo. Although it lay unmoving, its eyes were open and it did not seem to have sustained any obvious injury.

A fierce argument ensued. The village people demanded three hundred rupees (about forty dollars U.S. at that time) in payment for the offence to their buffalo. Chacko tried to explain that the team had no money whatsoever. The people were not sympathetic, and the men were praying desperately for a solution to this awkward situation when another vehicle drove up. One of the passengers in this vehicle, obviously a local person of high standing, inquired what the commotion was about. He saw that the OM team were strangers to the region and took pity on them. The calf was by no means dead, he pointed out. The sum the angry villagers were asking was unreasonable. After some bargaining the man succeeded in reducing their demand by 90% — to only thirty rupees. Although this was a great relief to the team, they still had no means of paying such a sum. Chacko boldly asked their kindly intercessor whether he would show them a further favor by leading them the money. The man could follow the team to their destination — a Finnish missionary's home not far away — where he would be reimbursed. Chacko intended to borrow the thirty rupees from the missionary.

Fortunately the gentleman agreed to this arrangement. He took the thirty rupees from his own pocket and the people were appeased. After a polite farewell, both vehicles drove off.

The Finnish missionary lady was expecting the team. As soon as she spotted the truck, she went inside and fetched a letter that had just arrived, addressed to Chacko. She greeted the men and handed Chacko the envelope. He was surprised, noting that it was from another OM team working a few hundred miles to the west. Inside was a money order for thirty rupees.

The accompanying note read: "We prayed for you this morning, and the Lord impressed it upon our hearts to send you these thirty rupees." The letter had been posted the previous week.

31

A Place for Us

by David Short

The months before the *Doulos* reached Tanzania, West Africa, three of us were sent out to make preparations. Our job was to meet with people in the shipping world, immigration and customs, education and government officials, as well as church leaders. We found a printer to deal with our publicity needs and formed a committee to organize the program. For many weeks we did little about a berth because the harbor authorities didn't allocate berths very far ahead of time. As we came into the last couple of weeks before the ship was due to arrive, however, our shipping agent informed us we had been assigned a berth right down at the end of the harbor.

It was a pleasant enough berth, even though the area was being developed and there was lots of reconstruction going on. The difficulty was that it was a long way out for visitors to travel. The harbor itself was already a mile or two out of the city center. On top of that, visitors would have to go an extra distance to our berth and there were no buses. This would probably mean arranging special transport.

We spent much time praying about this situation. Easy access is critical to the success of a ship visit, not only to attract crowds but also to provide facilities needed for daily operations.

One day we had lunch in a restaurant that overlooked the harbor. We felt led to pray again, and one of the team actually felt she should claim berth number One for the *Doulos*. This berth was right in front of the Harbor Master's office, the best place for people to get to and the easiest for ship transport needs.

Some time after that, I was riding with one of the ship committee members in his car. Thomas Masamu, who was in the pharmaceutical business, asked me what particular problems we were most concerned about. I wondered how much I should share, but decided to tell him about our prayers for berth number One.

"Well, that's quite remarkable," he responded, "Maybe I can help. I went to school with the Assistant Harbor Master. In fact, he comes from my village and is a member of my extended family line. Why don't we meet with him next Saturday morning and I'll introduce you?"

So we met with this official, and it turned out that it was his duty as Assistant Harbor Master to assign ships to their berths! By the end of our conversation he had agreed to give the *Doulos* berth number One.

I went to the shipping agent and told him the good news. He said that it was impossible. "Right now there's a Nigerian grain ship in that berth. The grain is being sucked out and pumped into storehouses day and night. This will take several more days, and the Doulos will get here before they're finished!"

The agent knew what he was talking about. We didn't understand how the Lord could give us the berth, but we carried on thanking Him in faith.

We were very busy during the last week before the ship's arrival. Right up to the final day, the grain ship was still occupying berth number One. But overnight, the port authorities moved that ship just enough to allow space for the *Doulos*. The great day came and she sailed in, right on time, and tied up alongside right where we had prayed she could.

The only problem came when we tried to put the gangways down. Two huge mobile cranes had rusted in place in the very spot we needed for the gangways. The cranes had been there about six years and wouldn't budge. Neither could our ship. But after some discussion the authorities were able to commandeer some tractors and heavy equipment to pull the cranes out of the way.

Many thousands came to the *Doulos* during the next two and a half weeks. We sold so many Bibles we ran out and had to re-order more in Swahili. At the end of the visit we went, as usual, to change the local currency we had gotten into international currency — U.S. dollars or German deutschmarks. There wasn't much time before the ship was due to sail but we got the business taken care of. Then the agent told us that we needed to get the signature of a certain individual in order to clear the ship for leaving port. Unfortunately this man wasn't in his office and no one knew where he was!

The Doulos's director was with me. Both of us were understandable anxious to get back and sail with the ship! So we prayed. And just then someone said, "I can't believe this. The man you need for a signature is walking right toward us, coming back to his office!"

We were warned that this man didn't like signing anything outside his office but we intercepted him. We asked if he would be kind enough to sign the paperwork there and then — and mercifully, he did. By that time, the director had gone on ahead. I had never made such a quick getaway in my life! The gangway was already dismantled as far as it could be before it was stowed on the side of the ship. As soon as I stepped aboard our ropes were cast off. Thanks to our Provider, it was another mission accomplished.

32

Special Delivery

by David Short

One time while I was with a ship line-up team in Manila, an urgent need arose to get some airplane tickets to Taiwan within 24 hours. Crew members on the *Doulos* in Taiwan needed those tickets to fly to England. When we contacted the express mail operators in the Philippines, however, none of them could guarantee delivery in 24 hours. In that part of the world there was always a chance of unforeseen delays.

After wondering what to do, we came up with the idea of taking the tickets to the airport and finding someone who could hand-carry them for us. The airport had strict security regulations that forbade entrance to anyone but passengers, but the administrator had given our team special passes. Two of us were able to walk right into the terminal and up to the check-in desk for Taiwan flights. There we stood praying silently and looking over the scores of people lining up to get on the plane. Which one should we approach?

Without consulting each other, we both chose the same individual. Of course it was awkward. We didn't know her and she didn't know us, and people are generally suspicious of being asked to carry anything onto the plane for someone else.

137

But this was important. We went up to this woman and after introducing ourselves explained the difficulty we were in. We then asked if she would be willing to help us get the tickets to Taiwan.

It was remarkable. First of all we learned that she often traveled between Taiwan and Manila — it sounded as though she, or both herself and her husband, were in business or connected to an embassy. She knew exactly where those tickets needed to be delivered in the Taiwan airport. She also spoke fluent Chinese, although she was from a European country, so she could explain to the agents what had to be done with the tickets.

The woman then asked, "What organization is this for?" When we showed her a picture of the ship and several leaflets, she exclaimed: "This is unbelievable!"

Just the previous night she had been with friends at a hotel, and they told her they had just visited the *Doulos* in Taiwan before flying to Manila. So the Lord had prepared her. She already knew about the ship and was ready to undertake our commission.

Shortly afterwards, this woman's flight took off. Within a few more hours our tickets were safely at their destination. To us, the whole incident was a wonderful example of God's timing and direction.

33

Do Romania Angels Drive Taxis?

by Jon Seeley

*L*ate one evening in the summer of 1991, I arrived home in Vienna, Austria and received a message from the Greater Europe team leader.

"We have a van load of humanitarian aid which is urgently required in Timisoara, Romania. Can you drive it in tomorrow?"

I agreed, and got a few hours sleep before lining up down at the Romania embassy first thing in the morning for a visa. I picked up the van and headed for the Hungarian border, armed only with the name and address of a Christian pastor in Timisoara, home of the Romania revolution. The pastor didn't even have a telephone, so there was no possibility of contacting him ahead of time for directions. I couldn't even be sure if he would be there when I arrived.

At the border I spent many hours wrangling with Hungarian and *Romania* customs officials. By the time I reached the outskirts of Timisoara, it was approaching midnight; pitch black, with most of the sparse street lights out of order.

I had already lost count of how many times I had narrowly avoided huge potholes, dogs, horses, carts and other unidentified objects on the unlit road since dusk. I had never visited this city before, and the map I had was of no use whatever, having been published with intentional errors as another example of the old regime's misinformation "security" ploys.

Waiting for morning wasn't a safe option. Even if I slept in the van, I could expect all moving parts to be stolen off the exterior — quite likely the contents as well. I had no way to defend my vehicle or its precious cargo of aid from the local Mafia. However was I to find my contact? I needed a miracle!

Anticipating this challenge right from the start of the trip, I had been praying throughout the long drive from Vienna. Maybe I should try to find a knowledgeable taxi driver. If he could understand my mix of stilted English/German he might be willing to help me locate my contact's house. Or, maybe he wouldn't....

Still on the outskirts of the city, I passed one of the few other vehicles on the road at that late hour. Suddenly I had a strange sense: *Perhaps that's the taxi I need!* It didn't even look like a taxi, but I slowed down and did a U-turn to "follow that car." As I did so, it stopped to let a passenger out! I pulled up nearby and tried my best to explain my request to the driver.

The man didn't say anything but smiled, nodded, and seemed to understand. I began to follow him through the darkened side streets, not sure whether he really knew where I wanted to go, or even whether he wanted to help or harm me! But God had given me a quiet confidence that He was in control of this situation. I followed along behind the taxi with a real sense of peace.

After only a short distance, the driver pulled up in a deserted side street. I got out to speak to him but he just pointed to one of the many unlit entrances of a nearby "communist block" of high-rise, high-risk flats. His gestures indicated "upstairs".

Assuming that this could be the place I needed to find, I offered the man some money for his trouble. To my great surprise he refused and drove off with a wave.

Now I was totally alone in an unknown suburb of a vast, post-communist city. Somewhere a long way down the road, a single street lamp valiantly flickered, casting eerie shadows under the trees. It provided just enough light to give the sense of one of those dreams where all the action is taking place just beyond your strangely obscured vision. I headed for the doorway and gingerly ventured from the dark street into the even darker stairwell. I groped my way up the stairs as carefully as I could, and when I got to the top of quite a few flights, I found what seemed to be a door. I knocked, quietly.

No answer. Questions began to snowball in my mind. Was this apartment remotely connected to where I wanted to be? Was my van where I had left it in the street below, or was all of this a simple ruse to get me away from it for a few minutes? And last but not, by far, least, *If I died here, would anyone who knew me ever find out about it?*

Just then I heard shuffling feet beyond the door. The door opened. *Yes!* This really was the pastor's apartment! After being offered a meal and warm tea, I drove the pastor across town and we dropped off the aid at the church. *Mission accomplished.*

A couple of hours later, I was safely crossing the border back into Hungary, en route for Vienna. My heart was full of thanks. And I couldn't help wondering then, as I still do: *"Is it really possible Romania angels drive taxis?"*

34

Berth-Day Presents

by Stan Thompson

When I was sent out to do line-up for the Logos in Lagos, Nigeria, I was immediately hit by the terrible congestion in the port. Nigeria had just recently discovered oil and come into sudden wealth. Not having had experience in handling such wealth, the government ministry responsible for building ordered a million tons of cement — *all at once!* Naturally, chaos ensued, since there was only one other major port in the country. Ships loaded with cement started arriving in Lagos and of course the port couldn't handle them all. When I arrived there were — without exaggeration — at least a hundred ships waiting at anchor to get in. Some had been waiting *nine or ten months.* Any captain arriving without prior permission would be clapped in jail, such was the seriousness of the situation.

I'm afraid I didn't have much hope for arranging a *Logos* visit. After much prayer, I went down to the office of the Chief Harbor Master. The man was Indian, not Nigerian, and quite friendly. He said to me: "You find a berth, and I'll tell you whether you can have it."

So I came out of his office. It was very hot and dusty; I was in a suit and didn't know my way around. There was a lot

143

of construction going on, including a major highway next to the water. I battled through all the dust of the trucks to the water's edge where there was a ferry terminal. I studied the place and saw that it was capable of berthing two ships. One had ferries coming and going all the time; the other was occupied by a ship by the name of the *Maris II*. I thought, *"If that thing wasn't there we could bring in the Logos."* It was right in the center and accessible to everything.

I went back to the Harbor Master's office. "I think I've found a place where we can berth the Logos II!" I told him.

He smiled. "Where is it?"

I described the berth. "The only problem is, the *Maris II* is there. How often is that ship in port?"

"Very often," he replied, "because it belongs to the Ministry of Transport. It's a survey vessel and only goes out every couple of months."

"That's the only place we could go. It's ideal for our purposes." I was praying all the time: *"Please, Lord, make this man sympathetic to our needs!"*

He said, "I'll tell you what. You go over to the Ministry of Transport and see the Superintendent. Tell him about your ship and if he agrees, I'll move the *Maris* further down the coast a little. We'll get a pile driver and drive some piles in so you can moor your ship there."

So I went back through the dust and heat, located the right office, and found myself confronted by a huge mountain of a man. As soon as I finished explaining the purpose of my visit, he exploded, *"Why should I allow your so-and-so ship to shift our ship?"*

He went on and on, finally blasting me out of the office. I returned to the Harbor Master's office with my tail between my legs, my heart thumping away. *"Oh, Lord,"* I was thinking, *"that didn't go so well. I pray that something can still be done!"*

The Harbor Master heard me out. He only said, "Well, just leave it to me, and I'll see what can be done."

Of course in the next few days I spent a lot of time praying. When I went back to the Harbor Master's office about a week later I learned that he had prevailed upon this captain to move the *Maris II!* The *Logos* came in to the ferry terminal and stayed there for the duration of her stay. It wasn't an ideal berth because of the heavy rise and fall of the tide — the mooring lines on the *Logos* kept wearing through and breaking. But it was just a miracle that we got in there at all!

My next assignment was to line things up in Port Harcourt, Nigeria. There were 'only' fifty ships at anchor there — and only three berths in the whole port. I went to our agent, a British company, and of course they said a *Logos* visit was impossible. There were no berths available. So off I trudged again, and just outside the port area I found a jetty for oil ships, like a catwalk. Some oil tanks were on the hill nearby.

Well, I thought, that's not very ideal. We couldn't bring any vehicles ashore. But it would be better than nothing. I went back to the agent and said to him, "I found a place that might work. I know it's impossible to get in the port, but this is outside the port and people could visit with no problem."

The superintendent shook his head. "I'm sorry, you can't go there." He opened a huge cargo plan and showed me there was a ship coming during the time the *Logos* planned to be in port. It was carrying tallow for the tanks I'd seen behind the berth. So, the man pointed out, it was out of the question.

That night I went to a prayer meeting being held at an Assemblies of God church. The place was packed with about 300 people. I shared the situation about the berth with the pastor and then the people all started praying aloud at the same time — the noise was terrific. I thought the roof was going to lift off the place!

I had already made contact with an honorary port chaplain (actually a nominal Christian), and asked him if he could help me get around a bit. He had a car, and I didn't know anyone at all in Port Harcourt. So he started taking me around to the customs and immigration and other offices. But one day he finally said to me, "I think it's disgraceful!"

"What is?" I asked, surprised.

"I think it's disgraceful you're wasting people's time, going around to all these offices and bothering them for permissions. You know jolly well that you can't get that ship in here. It's impossible!"

So I said, "Well, I'm awfully sorry that you see it that way. If you think I'm wasting *your* time, then perhaps I ought to find my own way around." And so I separated myself from his services and pressed on.

The key to the *Logos* getting a berth turned out to be the finance director of the port authority. This man had had a big alcohol problem, but he had been saved through the ministry of the Assembly of God church I'd attended. He had also been delivered of his alcoholism. It was this finance director who convinced the port authority that it would be far more beneficial to the community to allow the *Logos* to berth, than a commercial ship that was only out to make money.

That was how, when the *Logos* arrived, she got the berth I wanted outside the port. During our time there, the tallow ship duly arrived, but it had to anchor out with the other fifty ships outside the harbor. We were tied up the whole time and had a tremendous visit.

Our only problem with the berth was getting our vehicles off-loaded. Teams had been arranged to go inland so we needed the vans. Well, the same Assembly of God church had a member who worked in the public relations department of Shell Petroleum. Shell had a big refinery down the coast. He had me write a letter to his boss, appealing for help. And they sent a big, beautiful bow-loading barge, plus a tugboat, and brought them alongside the *Logos*. We used our ship's derricks to put the vans onto the barge, and the tug towed it into the beach where we could drive them off. The day we sailed they came again so we could re-load the vehicles. And it never cost us a penny!

35

How Many Pieces Of Luggage
Did You Say??

by Frank Fortunato

*I*n the mid-70's I was forced to spend some time at home recovering from injuries received in a devastating car crash, in which four other OMers were killed. After my recuperation I was invited to rejoin the ship *Logos* and continue my ministry with music and line-up. Certain charter flights from the United States that year allowed unlimited luggage. Being a good OMer I decided to take advantage of the special offer and packed a keyboard, keyboard amplifier, case of music books, typewriter, and other assorted equipment. In total I had seven pieces.

The ship was berthed in Istanbul, and my plan was to travel across Europe by train from Belgium. When I arrived at OM's Zaventem base, a leader asked if I could take some other supplies to the ship. I laughed and said I already had seven pieces. It then occurred to me that there was no way that I could personally handle seven pieces on my own. So if I had to have help for seven, I might as well use the same help to take more! I agreed to take them along. The leader then showed me eight suitcases waiting to get to the *Logos!* Among these were Christmas presents and other eagerly-anticipated mail. How could I say no?

Armed with fifteen pieces of luggage I set out for Istanbul. It was late December, so on the way I stopped for a wonderful Christmas with friends in the Vienna team. Then I continued on, passing through Hungary and reaching the Yugoslavia border in the middle of one fateful night. At this point a border guard asked me to open one of my bags. The sight of a whole suitcase stuffed with letters must have looked suspicious. The guard decided I had probably stolen the post and ordered me off the train. When he disappeared to check other passports, however, I decided there was no way I was getting off. Not at 2:30 a.m., in the middle of nowhere!

When the border guard returned and found me still on board, he snatched my passport from my shirt pocket and started punching me. The man was obviously serious, I had to get off the train – at once. Someone helped me off-load my luggage. Around 3 a.m. I watched the train pull away without me. There I stood on the platform with my fifteen bags, freezing cold. It was one of the most depressing and lonely moments of my life.

The policeman at the checkpoint still had my passport. He told me he would lock my gear in the customs room and send me back to Vienna later that morning. I refused to be separated from my bags, so he locked me in with them. At least the room was heated. A few hours later, around 6 a.m., I was let out. I walked boldly into the police station and demanded my passport, insisting that I had done nothing wrong. The man in charge flatly refused. I was to go back on the next train to Vienna, he said. I kept arguing with him, and finally he grabbed my passport and threw it across the platform. It landed on the tracks. I retrieved it gleefully. At last I would be able to continue on my way to Istanbul! I found a broken-down cart with three of its four tires flat and somehow managed to pile on all fifteen pieces of luggage and pull it to the edge of the platform. A train soon arrived and I loaded my precious cargo on board.

Around noon the train stopped again, somewhere inside Yugoslavia. After what seemed an unusually long wait I asked someone when the train was going to continue. He said the train was going nowhere. This was the end of the line! To my great dismay I was forced to unload all fifteen pieces, hire a porter and then find a hotel to accommodate me that day and night.

The next morning the same porter returned at 6 a.m. to help me get all my pieces back to the station. With relief I caught the next train, but this one proceeded only a few hours along the track before it, too, stopped. There had been a derailment ahead of us, we learned. It was going to take many hours of clearing the debris before we could proceed. My spirits plummeted. I was thirsty and hungry and I still had a long, long way left to go. Eventually I found two American hippies in one of the compartments and begged some sustenance. All they had was a bottle of whiskey! We eventually reached Istanbul twenty-four hours late, and to my great delight someone from the ship was there to meet me!

As we drove through the city to get to the port I noticed some banners strung along the street. Something about what it said looked familiar and I stared. The realization hit me. – That was my name on those banners! In shock, I asked the driver what the Turkish writing said. He told me that the ship's line-up man, Peter Conlan, was billing me as a famous American musician. The banners advertised a concert I was leading, with the *Logos* crew and staff, at a prominent hall in the city. I inquired, weakly, when this event was to take place. In four days, he said.

When I met Peter Conlan I wanted to wring his neck. Instead we concentrated for the next three days and nights on putting together a concert. And thanks be to the grace of God, everything turned out well. The evening proved a great encouragement, not only to our own staff but to other Christian workers in Istanbul. In a city where it wasn't allowed to openly preach the gospel, we were able to sing it loud and clear. And that – I have to admit – was worth hauling a hundred pieces of baggage across Europe!

HIS
SEEKING
TOUCH

36

A Matter of Life or Death

He was young. According to other people he had everything to live for. But to Diva life was simply "a long disease" that was best cured by death. The teenager found an isolated place and got out the two bottles of poison he had purchased. He drank both of them.

Divakaran T. was born into a family of high-caste Hindus. When he was only six, his teacher told his class the story of Jesus and how he was nailed to a cross. Divakaran cried when he heard this and later asked his mother why the people had to kill Jesus. He did not get a satisfactory answer.

Later on when he attended college, an English lecturer gave an eighty-minute talk on Christ's crucifixion, his subsequent resurrection and the Second Coming. In the college library Divakaran saw a magazine advertisement offering a free Bible correspondence course. He wrote in and received the first lesson as well as ten coupons to be distributed to friends, who might be interested in taking the course. When his friends wrote in, they too got ten coupons each. By the end of that year, 300 students at the college were doing the Bible Correspondence Course. Most of them were Muslims who were interested in improving their English.

Meanwhile, Divakaran was turning more and more to Hinduism to forget his family problems. Every morning he

155

faithfully spent half an hour in prayer and once he made a 45-mile pilgrimage through the jungle to a sacred temple. There he sat and fasted for fifteen days, hoping to gain merit. Still, he was dissatisfied. His devotion did not give him any inner peace, and he began to contemplate suicide.

At the age of 19, Divakaran traveled to New Delhi for the ostensible purpose of visiting a cousin. It was during this visit that he purchased poison to take his life. One day soon after, he came across an Operation Mobilization team selling Christian literature on the street. Diva bought a Bible and listened to what the men said about Jesus. But he had already made up his mind. Equipped with double the amount of poison he needed to kill himself, he left the city. *If Jesus is truly God and all-powerful,* was his last thought before drinking the deadly contents of the bottles, *then he will somehow intervene to save my life!*

Some time later, villagers spotted the teenager's still figure on the ground. They called the police, who rushed him to the hospital. The only address they could find was the one inside the Bible, belonging to the OM office. The police contacted the office. When team members visited the hospital, Divakaran was still unconscious. So they left a book under his pillow: Billy Graham's *Peace With God.*

When Divakaran opened his eyes, he realized immediately that his last desperate cry had been answered. Jesus truly was God. And he had cared about Diva enough to overrule his certain death. The young man read the book he found under his pillow, and prayed to receive God's forgiveness and peace. For the first time in his life he felt gloriously alive. After his discharge from the hospital, he went to stay with the OM team. One week led to another and eventually Divakaran joined OM He has now spent over twenty years sharing the love of God in every part of India. And he has had the supreme joy of introducing other members of his family to Jesus Christ — the Way, the Truth and the Life.

37

Ship of Dreams

by Debbie Meroff

Selina grew up in Taipei, Taiwan. Although her family were traditional Buddhists, she was introduced to Jesus Christ through a high school teacher, and later, a Christian camp. Selina decided to become a follower of Jesus, and became an enthusiastic witness to her friends. Her parents, however, reacted furiously. They considered their daughter's behavior an act of betrayal.

"My father told me we were Chinese and that we should worship our ancestors," explained Selina. "I think he was afraid I wouldn't pray for him when he died. He made me kneel in front of him. Then he slapped my face. I told him that the Bible says if you are slapped on one side; you must offer the other side, too; so I did. He was puzzled and disturbed."

After finishing high school, Selina worked in her father's hardware business for several years. "He gave me a hard time," she recalls with emotion. "I cried a lot. Every Sunday when I wanted to go to church, he would argue. It was as though he thought since I believed in Jesus, I didn't belong to him any more."

Selina continued to pray that God would give her some way to serve Him. One night she had a strange dream. In it she saw a white ship, surrounded by singing and light.

"I asked God what it was all about, and He said, *'That's where you should go!'* So I started looking for a ship. I had never heard of one anything like that. Then, while I was in a Youth for Christ office one day, I saw a brochure about the Doulos. I knew at once that that was the ship I was looking for! I got in touch with the OM office, even though I didn't think my father would let me go."

Soon afterward, Selina and her father went to Shanghai on business for a month. Her father owned a factory in the city and visited frequently. She asked him while they were there if she could go to a church on Sunday. At first he refused, but then he said he would take her and wait outside.

"But after waiting a few minutes that day he went inside, too. He told me later that he had had a dream a few nights before. He heard a voice say to him, *'Don't try to stop your daughter from doing what she wants.'* He was shaken by that dream. He told me he would agree if I still wanted to go to the ship. But he also added angrily, 'Let God take care of you, I won't any more!'

"I joined the *Doulos's* six-month volunteer program in Subic Bay, Philippines, during the summer of 1996. I didn't know why God wanted me on the ship. Now, I believe it was for my family's sake."

Selina's father had no idea when the Doulos would be visiting Shanghai, or if he would be there at the same time. He had been traveling back and forth from Taiwan for six years. But when the *Doulos* reached Shanghai, he was there.

Selina smiled: "I wanted to show my father that I had a big God! On the *Doulos* there are so many people from so many countries, all believing in Him! My father couldn't come to the ship because the public wasn't allowed, but we arranged for about thirteen *Doulos* people from ten countries to visit his factory. When he asked Kenny Gan to pray, I was very excited. My father would never admit anything to me, because that would be losing face after all those years of opposition — but I knew his heart had changed."

When the *Doulos* reached Taiwan the following October, Selina left the ship of her dreams. Her mission was accomplished. And she had no doubt whatsoever that God had the next step planned, as well.

38

Go Tell It on the Mountains!

The three men had stopped only briefly in a tiny, remote village high in the Atlas Mountains of North Africa. A chance meeting led to sharing the good news of Jesus with a villager. Before the team moved on, they gave him a copy of Luke's gospel. He thanked them and left quickly. Soon he was back with several of his friends. They, too, wanted a copy of this book, they said. The team obliged and each man went on his way, smiling.

After the three left the village, they split up, Harry went in one direction and Jon and Caleb in another. The latter had walked about a kilometer when they heard a rattling sound behind them. Turning, they saw an old man slowly pedaling his bike along the bumpy mountain road. He pulled up next to the young men and exchanged the long, customary greetings of the region. Then the old fellow got to the point.

"Do you have any Injils (Gospels or New Testaments)?" he asked expectantly.

To their chagrin, the pair discovered that Harry had, by mistake, taken all of the books on his detour to another village. Caleb explained that the man would have to collect it from them in the next town that evening, when they expected Harry to rejoin them. The old man pedaled off, disappointed.

That night the team reunited and went to eat their dinner in a little café in the heart of the town. They had not been able to talk to anyone about the Lord in this place. Just then, however, their waiter placed a serviette in front of Jon. There was something scrawled on it in French. Jon translated the words for the others: *"Do you have a New Testament?"*

The grapevine in these mountains was obviously very effective. Caleb slipped the book to the waiter as inconspicuously as possible. One sharp-eyed man a few tables away noticed the transaction, however. A few moments after the waiter had left, "eagle-eye" stood up and approached the three men. He smiled and gave his greetings while the men tensed. Then he said, in an undertone, "I saw you give the Injil to the waiter. Do you have two more? — one for myself and one for my friend?" The four men talked until it grew late. Before they left the café, their new acquaintance was in grateful possession of the books he'd asked for.

And the old man Jon and Caleb had met on the trail? Out of the dark he squeaked on his ancient bicycle. He managed to find the three foreigners and triumphantly collected his "prize." It turned out the man was a circuit-riding Imam (local Koranic teacher) who had been listening to Christian radio broadcasts. He wanted to find out more about the Messiah.

39

Higher Authority

by Lawrence Hebb

I began working in UN-occupied Northern Iraq in 1993. The team had already been there two years, since the Gulf War, helping the Kurds with relief and development projects. Most of the Kurdish people are nominal Muslims. In all of their history they have had very little exposure to followers of Jesus Christ. Now, through the practical testimony of Christian relief workers, some were coming to faith.

One day one of the other workers in Zakho came to us with the idea of showing the *Jesus* film in one of the main areas of town. Without too much praying about it we said yes. We really wanted to see these people come to know Jesus.

When the appointed evening came, we set off with the equipment and our usual guards (as foreigners we were required by UN rules to take armed guards wherever we went) and began setting up.

Soon people started to cluster around and ask what we were doing. When we replied we were going to show a film they were happy.

"Hope it's a good one, like Rambo!"

"Well," we replied, "it's a good film but not Rambo."

"Well, never mind. Terminator is also good."

"Actually, this film isn't about violence."

"Oh! Then what is it about?"

"The life of Jesus."

"YOU CAN'T SHOW THAT FILM HERE!"

To cut a long story very short, we learned that we were talking to members of the leading Islamic party. They made it clear that if we tried to show the film they would bring out their guns, shoot up the equipment and probably us as well. At this point, the team really began to pray. We knew these were not idle threats. Almost every man and boy in Kurdistan carried weapons. Grenades were sold in the market place. But if we backed down now we would never be able to do any kind of outreach in the open again. These Muslims knew they had us, but we really felt that the Lord didn't want us to quit. The local parties who were in charge in Northern Iraq had given their blessing to the film and it had even been shown on local TV. So we prayed and continued to set up.

As we got nearer to starting time, the Muslims came back with even more threats. There were about 300 people now waiting to see the film, so we prayed even harder for God to intervene.

We started the projector and it looked certain there would be serious trouble. Voices began to rise in protest. Just then, along came half a dozen Kurdish soldiers. Seeing that something was going on, they asked which film was about to be shown. These men were well armed. We didn't know what to do so we simply told them it was the Jesus film. We fully expected these soldiers would tell us to pack up. Instead, to our astonished wonder, their leader nodded approvingly. "Oh yes, that's a great film," he said, and his group settled down to watch it.

The troublemakers realized that to disrupt the film at this point would not go over well with the local authorities. They promptly disappeared.

That night nearly 400 Kurds saw the Jesus film in their own language. I wish I could say that a lot of them came to know Jesus, but there's just no way of telling. One thing I do know is that those people had the chance to respond to the gospel for the first time in their lives. That's enough for me.

40

Written on the Wind

by Chacko Thomas
as told to Anne Buchanan Kammies

One day while the ship Logos was berthed in Jakarta, Indonesia, in 1973, two vans filled with crew members headed for the mountains. The team was all members of an Intensive Training Program who were planning to hold special meetings in the town of Bandung. The journey was a long one. When they found themselves passing through a number of villages along the way, they decided to make the most of it. They started throwing tracts out of the windows.

There was a certain skill involved in this. With practice it was possible to fling a pile of tracts upward so they would float down in a wide, evenly spread area — hopefully straight into the eagerly up-stretched hands of the waiting people! As the team traveled through the towns the leaflets were flying freely. By the time they reached their destination they had probably distributed thousands.

Thinking no more about it, the team members proceeded with their ministry in Bandung. A few days later, however, they received an unexpected visitor — a very excited headmaster! This man had an amazing story to tell, so amazing that he had spent the last day or two earnestly tracking down the team. He wanted to share his joy with them.

The headmaster was one of very few Christians in the area, living in one of the villages the ship vans had passed through on their way to Bandung. A few mornings before, he had waked up to discover he had visitors urgently waiting to speak to him — twenty-three visitors to be exact! The people were all from different homes and families in the village. Each one proceeded to tell him of a vivid dream they had just had. All 23 had exactly the same experience of hearing a voice clearly tell them, *"Go and see the headmaster. Ask him to explain the message on the tract you received. Otherwise you will perish."*

There and then the headmaster carefully explained the way of salvation to his eager Muslim audience. Immediately they accepted Christ. They wanted to be baptized.

The headmaster was overwhelmed. So was the team as, with tears streaming down his face, the man related his incredible story. For only then did they realize how much they had underestimated the love of God.

41

By Appointment Only

by Rowan Clifford
(pseudonym used for security reasons)

ack home, I used to be a carpenter. I enjoyed my job.
But nothing can beat the thrill of being an agent for
God in a "closed" Islamic country.

Every day, somewhere in the vast metropolis of Casablanca – and all over Morocco for that matter – people are hearing the gospel message over the radio. Some are sending away to schools in Europe for evangelistic-type lessons. They do this in secret. After someone has studied for a while and has shown a degree of openness, their address is discreetly passed on to me. It now becomes my task to contact him and set up a rendezvous. A trusted friend writes the letter for me in Arabic, explaining I am a foreigner, a friend of the correspondence school, and I would like to meet him. I pick a crowded public place where we can meet and advise him to hold my letter in his hand. You may think that this is overdone, that I have read too many spy novels. But both foreigners and Moroccans have gone to jail because of such meetings and I have already been a guest of one Arab government for three days. Once is enough!

On the appointed day and hour I arrive at our meeting point: a bus station. It's crowded and people are moving about. The perfect environment. I am dressed in the most Moroccan-looking clothing I own: a black jacket, bright mustard yellow trousers and casual shoes. I am a bit early and lean against a wall, looking for my man. Why does everyone look like an undercover cop? I try not to look as if I'm doing anything illegal. A feeling from the old days – when I wasn't such a nice Christian boy and was trying not to get caught by the police – comes back. My contact is a little late. A clean-shaven man walks by, wearing a brightly-colored shirt, trousers and dark sunglasses. Maybe he forgot the envelope. I look for someone who looks like he might be looking for someone. It's a bit confusing. I pray some more. I glance at my watch for the hundredth time to show that I am waiting for someone.

A young guy slowly edges onto the scene. He is wearing a running suit and thongs, looks unshaven and very thin. He looks around, then asks someone for the time. Instinct tells me it's him. From his pocket he slides out the envelope and nervously looks around some more. I go up and say hello, and we simultaneously heave a sign of relief.

Later, he tells me that he has spent the last week in fear, wondering if my letter was a trap from the police, or was it a joke? We sit down in a coffee shop. I'm hoping he isn't just trying to get a visa out of the country from all this. He's hoping I'm not with a dangerous political movement. The last thing he wants is to visit the secret police's notorious "Villa Rouge" and have 220 volts run through his body. Open-heartedly he wants to know more about the gospel. He tells me that for two years he has been waiting to find out more about Jesus. This is just the start. For our next meeting I will take with me a Moroccan friend who is already a believer. Many of the established believers became Christians in this way.

We part. It's been another successful mission. I wonder how many more men and women are waiting, like this man. Maybe they have waited a lifetime. My heart is full. One thing is sure: God knows what He's doing. He has it all worked out.

OM Literature is a literature ministry of Operation Mobilization, an international missions organization with ministries in over eighty nations of the world. Founded in 1957, the ministry has grown from a handful of students to approximately 3000 full time workers and an additional 4000+ short term volunteers annually from all over the world.

Your Part in World Missions

You may be asking where you, as a Christian, fit into God's plan for the salvation of the world. Here are a few ways you can beinvolved now!

YOU CAN PRAY — Get informed about God's world. Ask for information about missionaries in areas of particular interest to you. Stand before God on behalf of your brothers and sisters on the mission field. Pray for more missionaries to be called and sent to reach the lost for Christ. Don't be surprised if God uses you to answer your own prayers.

YOU CAN GIVE — God has given you the privilege of being responsible for a portion of His money. Decide how much you can keep for yourself, then use the rest to further God's kingdom. One way is to support foreign mission work.

YOU CAN SEND — Look around in your church or community. Seek out another who senses a call to mission, then spur him on and encourage him to further seek God's direction for his life. Adopt a missionary. Give him moral support. Encourage him through letters or tapes; let him know that you believe in him and in the work God has called him to. Maybe you are in the position to offer him a place to stay or a car to use while he's on home assignment.

YOU CAN GO — The Great Commission is a call to you too! You can see the need. Why delay?

Contact us if you want to know more:

**OM Literature,
P.O. Box 1047,
129 Mobilization Drive
Waynesboro, GA 30830-2047, U.S.A.**